CUBAN BLUES

I was labeled prisoner No. 48127. This photo was taken just two months after we were captured, and shortly after my first haircut and shave. My outlook was grim.

CUBAN BLUES

How Captivity in a Foreign Prison Saved My Life

Gordon Louis Hesse

PRECOCITY PRESS

Editor: Brenda Lange
Creative Director and Cover Designer: Susan Shankin
Book Design and Layout: Susan Shankin
Front Cover Image: Gordon Hesse's self-portrait soon after returning to the U.S.
Precocity Press, Los Angeles, CA

Author's Note: This book is a memoir based on the author's recollection of experiences over time, and quotations are sometimes reconstructed from the author's memory. While the book is a work of nonfiction, some names and identifying details have been changed and some events have been compressed. The author recognizes that participants' recollections of the events described herein may differ from his own, but every effort has been made to evoke what the author saw and heard with the greatest possible accuracy.

ISBN: 979-8-9909460-3-3 Trade paperback
ISBN: 979-8-9909460-4-0 eBook

Library of Congress Control Number: 2024916875
First edition printed in the United States of America

I dedicate this book in honor of my parents, Louis and Carol Hesse and my son, Louis Conor Kanon Hesse. They each, in their own way, have provided guidance, kindness, and inspiration and set high standards for me as I continually strive to be a better person.

CONTENTS

CAPTURE: MAY 26, 1973

I was 25 years old and standing naked on the stern deck of the *Silver Sands,* washing the salt and diesel fuel out of my hair with a hose. I had spent the last two hours on the rust-stained and aging shrimp boat pumping fuel from 55-gallon drums into the vessel's tanks and securing loose rigging. If all went well, our destination was Jamaica, but we had been having problems with the navigation gear. It didn't help that we had little experience.

The sky to the south was an angry soot color; a storm was imminent. A passenger ship cruised idly about a half mile to the north. I became self-conscious about the possibility of someone—or a group—bored with ship deck activities, watching my shower through binoculars. I began to feel uncomfortable. It was May 26, 1973.

As I wiped the soap from my eyes, I looked west toward the setting sun and saw the menacing silhouette of a gunboat, its bow framed in white streams headed straight for us. In that instant, I could feel my blood surge in fear. It had to be a Cuban vessel. Cuba then was the Soviet Union's Communist foothold in the Western Hemisphere. This renegade nation, run by the strong arm of Fidel Castro and his revolutionary spawning presence, had been a nemesis to four U.S. presidential administrations.

I looked around the cabin in the direction we were headed in our lumbering vessel. I could see the ghostly purple Sierra Maestras—perhaps 20 miles away.

Worse though, I could see shacks on a small island. The windows and doors on the huts were discernible. We were too close to shore.

Shit!

My mind raced through all the news footage I had seen on television as an impressionable adolescent during the late 1950s. I recalled how Fidel and a small band of guerillas had fought against the forces of military strongman Fulgencio Batista.

Through a military coup, Batista seized control of Cuba in 1952. A year later, Fidel led a failed attempt to start a popular uprising, was imprisoned, released in 1955 and returned the next year with a band of fewer than 100 soldiers. They used guerilla tactics to win popular support and control of the island nation, province by province, and marched triumphantly into Havana on New Year's Day, 1959. Shortly thereafter, Fidel transformed Cuba into a one-party Socialist republic with the Soviet Union during the Cold War and became an anathema to the U.S., which had tried to overthrow him many times, most publicly with the failed Bay of Pigs invasion in April 1961.

It was obvious the Cubans were likely to find us to be suspicious—maybe even provocative. These thoughts went streaming through my head as I returned my gaze to the gunboat. It was bearing down fast and growing more malevolent by the moment. I could make out the heavy machine guns that could turn our cabin into splinters in seconds.

"Cal, turn the boat out to sea!" I yelled to the wheelhouse.

I looked down the stern hatch to the engine room and saw Chet, the skipper, dressed in jeans and a greasy T-shirt where I had left him just 10 minutes earlier, with a wrench in hand, massive ear protectors on and checking fuel connections. A year older than I, he had a ruddy complexion and stood six feet tall. Except for his thick reddish-blonde hair and blue eyes, we were similar in build and appearance. Above the roar of the diesels, I shouted, "Chet, we've got trouble. A gunboat is coming up on us!"

With the hammering of the big diesel engines and the hearing protector headset he was wearing, he couldn't hear what I said, but my expression was loud enough for him to understand. When I pointed to the west, he scrambled up the ladder to the stern and saw the gunboat. Now we could make out the helmeted crew at their machine-gun battle stations. Built for speed, the gunboat's hull split the water into a V, shooting translucent sheets to its sides. The crew all had their orange life jackets on. Two of them motioned that we should turn out of their waters.

All of a sudden, I felt my nakedness and ran inside to grab pants, bumping into a befuddled Dan, the fourth member of the crew, who had been awakened by the shouts. With his light curly hair going in all directions and snaking over his ears and neck, he looked even more bewildered.

The previous evening when we were both off shift, Dan had offered to share a joint. It was an exceptionally tranquil twilight. We climbed up on the cabin roof while our vessel motored south smoothly over the sea that seemed like a sensual ribbon of light. I took a few hits, and the grass made the night seem even more stunning as the stars began to show themselves. At one point, as I was star gazing and looking for constellations, I saw the light reflected off a satellite as it traveled across the full moon. Like the appearance of a comet, it seemed to be an omen. It was to be the last evening of peace for a long time.

"Dan, you better get rid of that grass we were smoking last night. If they board us and find it, they'll have reason to hold us."

His bushy Fu Manchu mustache framed the firm set of his jaw, confirming he understood the seriousness of the situation as he returned to the cabin to find his small stash.

I hopped into my pants and jabbed my head and arms through a shirt as Chet rushed to the radio. He was going to send a distress signal. But the radio had been turned off earlier in the day when we had anchored near an atoll off Bermuda, and we had never turned it back on. It would take precious minutes for the vacuum tubes to warm up—not enough time!

As I went out to the deck, the Cuban gunboat slowed and pulled alongside our boat.

Their faces were distinct. Men on the bow and amidships were throwing lines to tie up to us. In two minutes, the vessels were secured to one another, and a boarding party of eight men armed with rifles and led by an officer with a holstered sidearm came on board. The leader tried to talk to us in Spanish. Although I had studied the language throughout high school, in the panic I was hard-pressed to remember the most basic expressions beyond "How are you?" and "It is raining."

As a few members of the Cuban crew searched our vessel, the remainder stayed poised at their guns. During their first sweep of the vessel, they found a pistol and a small caliber rifle, military surplus—including a fatigue jacket—Swiss Army and Buck knives, a grey, metal Navy case and a waterproof, military neoprene bag.

The sun was out of sight. On an evening when the onset of twilight could have been a thing of wonder and beauty, I felt a deep, dank gloom.

After a preliminary search of our vessel revealed no immediate threat in our demeanor or cargo, the tension among the soldiers eased, and the mood and exchanges became more informal. The captain of the gunboat even leafed through our book on navigation, then gave a patronizing smile to his comrades to indicate he thought we were inexperienced seamen—mere rookies, way out of our depth. We were told that the Cuban boat would remain secured to us until the approaching storm and night had passed.

Most of his crew left our vessel and two sentries were left on the *Silver Sands*. The gunboat remained tied up to us as darkness fell and the storm drew closer. The electrical charge in the air had an emotional and psychological effect as undeniable as it was physical. The mood was one of ominous foreboding, added to by the hair on our arms rising from the ionized molecules. The short-wave radio on the gunboat crackled with static as the gunboat's crew relayed their findings and received orders.

An eerie blue glow emanated from the electrically charged masts and the gantries of the net outriggers. It was St. Elmo's Fire—hissing and heightening this surreal experience.

All this time, we had been preoccupied with the Cuban search team and bracing for the storm. Conversation between us was minimal as each of us was lost in thought about how our circumstances were changing by the minute.

I drew this image of the Cuban gunboat from memory about a year after returning to the U.S. The sketches done after I was released were a way of processing the traumatic events.

When the storm hit, the wind, waves and rain came hard and fast. Both of the vessels rocked, the lines tying them together creaked as they stretched and strained close to the snapping point. The hulls groaned against each other as the gunnels rubbed like lovers in passionate throes.

Within half an hour, the storm had passed, followed by a dead calm and smothering humidity. Chet and I talked about our circumstances. Slightly reassured by the captain that we would be free to go in the morning, we opted not to try sending a radio message out since a sentry was posted on our vessel. I was to realize only later that our movements and appearance were being perceived as those of a paramilitary operation.

Dan was left on wheel watch as the rest of us, exhausted, tried to get a little sleep and prepare for the morning. I was restless and slipped in and out of consciousness as the water lapped at the hull of our vessel and fear lapped at my heart.

The radio crackled static and shattered Spanish throughout the night.

QUESTIONING: MAY 27, 1973

The situation worsened in the morning when the Cubans said we'd be taken into port for further questioning.

It was becoming apparent that this was not going to be simple or short, even though they assured us they would only detain us "a day or two—just cautionary procedures and formalities." The Cubans left two soldiers on our boat as we motored behind the gunboat along the coast.

My thoughts turned to news reports, rumors and investigations about the numerous attempts that had been made on Fidel Castro's life: snipers, poisonings, exploding cigars and other explosive devices. Lee Harvey Oswald, the alleged assassin of President John F. Kennedy, had mysterious links to Cuba. Some thought his actions were to have been Castro's retaliation.

We cruised into a cove that led to the fishing village of Nuevitas, not far from the city of Camaguey. As we came into the dock, a small crowd of about two dozen people gathered around. Most of them seemed to be low-ranking soldiers, curious field workers and other gawking locals. In front of all of them were two men wearing cheap sunglasses. We met these new handlers who had the the bearing of detectives and high-level security officers, complete with hard-set and chiseled faces. They took complete control and there were no pleasant exchanges. I felt like we were spinning into a whirlpool, getting drawn down faster by the minute.

"You will be able to resume your voyage after the boat has been fumigated," the taller, heavyset man said. My stomach churned and I foresaw grave hours, if not days or weeks, ahead. These feelings were only compounded when our crew was separated and distributed in four shiny new vehicles with Cuban Department of the Interior insignias on the doors.

I sat wordlessly for 30 minutes as the caravan drove at breakneck speed over dirt roads, kicking up clouds of dust as we passed along the seashore weeds and sugarcane fields, through villages that were little more than a sprinkling of buildings. We passed billboards with Che Guevarra's image and slogans like *Venceremos o Muerte* (We will have victory or death). The roads led us to a small, sprawling city, which we later learned was Camaguey, where the largest buildings were only three stories high. After a series of tight turns, we pulled into a walled villa that appeared to be an administrative compound with several guards on the perimeter. Guards also were posted at the entrance gates that closed after our vehicles entered.

We were told not to talk with one another and were put into two separate rooms. Dan and I were directed to hardwood chairs in a large living room with 14-foot ceilings. Two young guards, probably still in their teens, watched us for the next few hours. I had the distinct feeling they were taking their time with us to "soften" us up or to await the arrival of a higher official. We left our chairs only to eat lunch together, almost wordlessly, speaking only when we needed something to drink or to go to the *baño*. Over the next few days we would be called in, one by one, and questioned about our actions in the days preceding our capture by the Cuban gunboat.

We spent a week there. Each day we sat in hard chairs, two to a room—all day—except for meals. Eight hours a day sitting in those chairs didn't qualify as torture, but it was a mild form of torment. They began their questioning with Chet.

Most of the questions I was asked were about my employment. And why had I not done military service? The inference was that I was a specialist who was performing an alternative service, perhaps as a clandestine operative for an organization like Alpha 66.

Established in Puerto Rico in 1961, shortly after Fidel seized power, Alpha 66 took its name from the first letter of the Greek alphabet, referring to the beginning of the fight against Communism in Cuba. The original group was composed of 66 men, many who had fought against the Batista dictatorship. It was created, according to its promotional literature, with the intention of making commando attacks on Cuba "to maintain the fighting spirit of the Cuban people after the failure of the Bay of Pigs."

After 1962, a series of attacks were made on Cuban ports and G-2, Castro's dreaded military police. Alpha 66 initiated infiltrations and attacks in Matanzas Bay, the port of Havana and elsewhere. It even initiated the "Omega Plan," which consisted of situating a guerrilla force inside Cuba, but the attempts failed.

I was also asked about the atoll we had anchored at a few hours before the gunboat came upon us. They wanted to know what we had placed on the island. We had anchored and shut down the vessel's engines and electrical systems to check the hull, rudder and props to make sure everything was clear. We also used the opportunity to float a hatch cover (that we had been tripping over) to the island where it would not float into the hull of another vessel. I couldn't figure out what they were doing, but it confirmed my suspicion that a boat was spying on us. It had followed a parallel course to ours for two days before our capture. Now even the most innocent items on our vessel began to take on a sinister character.

I later learned how serious our situation had gotten when Chet had the chance to tell me about his questioning. He said he was brought into a room where several items from the vessel were laid out on a table. Three unidentified people were in the room, two sitting slightly behind Chet and to his side. The one in front began asking him about several of the items: guns, knives, walkie-talkies, and then, strangely, he showed a puzzling interest in the 8-track tape player, tapes and headphones.

Chet was asked what the tape player was for. He figured because it was a Third World country, they had probably never seen such technologically sophisticated devices. This was, after all, the early 1970s. Chet explained that, like many work boats, the mechanism was to play music over speakers when the crew was working on deck. The headphones made it possible for the guy at the helm to listen without disturbing the rest of the sleeping crew. Working vessels were commonly outfitted with such inexpensive systems to lift the spirits of the crew during the long cruises to and from port and to take their minds from backbreaking toil.

The inquisitor then pointed to the box filled with 8-track tapes with titles by bands like Grand Funk Railroad and the Allman Brothers.

"What are these?" he squealed with a sweep of his hand over the box of tapes.

"They're tapes; they go in like this," Chet said, showing how to insert the bulky cartridge into a slot in the machine. "See, like this, and they play music."

"All of them?" the inquisitor asked in a rising tone.

"Yeah," Chet said.

Then, with a dramatic flair, the inquisitor reached behind his back, pulled out a tape cartridge and sardonically shrieked, "What about this one?"

The inquisitor's tone implied he believed Chet had been caught in a web of incriminating evidence through his brilliant logic.

He was holding the head cleaner cartridge.

The head cleaners wiped away microscopic gunk and metal particles that accumulated on the magnetic tape. The cleaners at that time only had bleeps on them that played every other second. You would put the tape in, let it play until it bleeped three or four times and remove it. The magnetic heads were then supposed to be as shiny as polished silver. In the Cubans' paranoid minds, these bleeps could only be micro-coded instructions or data. While we associated the headset with the luxury of listening in private, they thought it was military gear. Could it be a device with audio microdots with which we were communicating with the manned Skylab, which had been launched a week earlier and orbited above Cuba every 90 minutes?

They also asked about the money hidden in the fuel tank: $20,000. It was something I knew nothing about. Our goose was cooked.

MEMORIES: MAY 28, 1973

I sat on the hard chair in silence day after day, waiting to find out what outcome awaited us.

I was preoccupied by fear, tedium, doubts and discomfort. It was inevitable that I would ponder the extremely good fortune, if not material wealth, of my life.

I was the youngest of three children born to Carol and Louis Hesse, middle-class parents who had worked hard to provide for their children. For much of my life, they had each worked two jobs so they could help send us all to college for the opportunities they didn't have because of the Depression. I had two sisters, eight and three years older than I.

Looking back, I began to realize how fortunate I had been. Despite the long hours my parents worked, I never lacked their attention or affection.

Both of my parents were gifted athletes. My mother won diving competitions, and my father played on championship high school baseball and basketball teams. Although he attended Lehigh University for only two years, as a pitcher on the varsity baseball team, he had the distinction of never losing a game. He was modest about it, saying any time he gave up a lot of runs, another pitcher would come in and turn the game around or his team would start hitting in runs. He loved sports and I know it pleased him whenever I played Little League or tried out for basketball, baseball and football teams.

When I was little, my dad worked on Greenwich Street in New York City selling centrifugal pumps. Back in the early 1950s, the area around his office seemed like a community of neighborly importers, businessmen and restaurants. A few times I traveled in on the train with him—probably when my mother was tied up with projects or doing something special with my older sisters. I recalled him proudly showing me off to his fellow workers and taking me to the coffee shop, and even the barber. The kindness and interest they showed me made me feel he was looked upon with affection: if I was "Lou's kid," I must be special. Early on, I felt important—maybe even a little bit different—perhaps because my father was held in such high regard for his honesty, fairness and kindness.

One of the first stops when we arrived in the city was at Jimmy's Diner. Jimmy and his one waitress showered attention on my father and me—a small boy who drank in the clinking sounds of dishes being cleared and the grill sizzling, the smells of strong coffee and bacon and the array of faces. Strangers and regular customers all greeted me with smiles, and I knew it was because my father was friendly to all.

During the day we passed a few panhandlers—the first I had ever seen. I didn't know what to make of the people asking for money. My father walked past them. A few steps later, perhaps sensing his uncharacteristic detachment, he told me they would usually ask for money for food. He said he would not give them money, fearing it would be used for alcohol or drugs, but if they really needed food, he would see that they got fed.

He would tell them to go to Jimmy's and say, "Lou Hesse said he'd pay for my meal." The people at the diner knew him and knew that he would pay the bill. My dad told me that Jimmy never once said that anyone came in asking for a meal or mentioning my dad's name. My father said either none of them was interested in food because they wanted booze—or Jimmy never bothered to keep track, figuring if my father vouched for them, it was an act of charity for all.

My dad's office was little more than a dozen feet wide and four times as long, with one window at either end. Old motors and rotors, small boxes, belts and tools were nearly everywhere. The smell of machine oil seemed to ooze from the dark wood of the floor and shelves.

At that age, more than an hour or two of me being in that setting, and with a child's typically short attention span, I would have begun to distract him. I'm sure he felt neglectful of his small son—so much so that he wasn't getting much work done. It was probably then that we went out to visit more of the community surrounding Greenwich Street. We walked down by the point of Manhattan and looked at the tugboats, the ocean liners, the Statute of Liberty and the ferries cruising the mouth of the Hudson River. We walked to a market area with large, fixed awnings. Nuts and seeds from all over the world were for sale in big wooden barrels. The manager knew my father and handed me a big scoop and a bag and told me to dip nuts out of any of the barrels. There were almonds, peanuts, macadamia, salt—coated and plain sunflower seeds, pistachios, brown and green nuts, and one pink kind. I filled the bag and discovered I liked the salt-covered sunflower seeds best.

My father probably decided to call it a day to beat the rush hour crowd. We went to the station and headed home, with me reaching into the bag and looking out the window at the passing industrial and urban landscape before the train took us within two blocks of our home.

Although we lived in Roselle Park, New Jersey, when I started elementary school, we spent all our summers at our home at the Jersey

Shore. Lavallette is only a mile long, situated on a barrier peninsula, with Barnegat Bay on the west side and the Atlantic Ocean on the east. During the summer it was teeming with vacationers, surf fishermen and boaters; in the winter, it became a ghost town. In the 1950s, when I was about to enter second grade, my parents thought raising their children in Lavallette would provide a more wholesome environment farther from urban influences, so we stayed after our summer neighbors and the tourists left.

Our home was several hundred feet from the beach. With the windows open, I could lie in my bed at night and be lulled to sleep listening to the waves breaking on the beach.

In the late summer and fall weekend evenings, I would tag along with my father when he took his long, surf-fishing rods and reels to the beach, and cast for bluefish, weakfish, striped bass and flounder. Back then, it was not uncommon to see fishermen in wading boots as far as the eye could see along the shoreline. I'd play in the sand until the light dwindled and the stars appeared, then I'd lie on my back and marvel at the large, deep and dark night sky. I'd look for constellations, not find them and make up my own. I'd wonder about what my life would be like, who I'd become, and what I would do in life. What places would I see? Who would become my friends or my wife?

Several times these daydreams were interrupted by a hue and cry that would start in the distance and get closer. Excitement would reign as a school of fish made its way along the coastal shallows. On more than one occasion, I remember my father casting so hard that he would snap a lure and race to thread the line through the eyes of the pole and tie on a new lure before the school passed. Usually, he was too late.

One Sunday night after a church youth group meeting, my father took me to the beach, excitedly showing me the effects of a tide of phosphorescence that made the breaking waves glow in the autumn dark. It had saturated the sand along the water's edge, and at each step, a circle of light glowed eerily around the pressure of each foot. It added new magic to living at the edge of the sea.

Back in the 1950s, there were few television stations to watch—perhaps there were three or four—and antenna reception from New York or Philadelphia was filled with static by the salty air.

For amusement in the nearly empty town, when my parents felt I was responsible and old enough, they would let me beachcomb alone after school before I settled in to do homework. I'd look for the wonders that washed up along the shore and developed an ability to spot anomalies. I'd collect bottles, sea glass, colorful stones and shells, starfish, seahorses, unusual bottles and driftwood. Once I'd even come home with a grebe—a diving bird of the cormorant family—that had gotten tangled in fishing line and tar and could no longer fly.

I'd study the waters and the moods of the ocean when it was at peace and gently lapped over the sandbars or in the aftermath of storms when the waves had the power of thunder and swift currents ate away at the sandy beaches. I witnessed the devastating power when the relentless, massive waves struck bulkheads with so much force they splashed higher than two-story homes and ate away at luxury oceanfront houses that would slide and crumble into the surf.

I'd watch the fishing and luxury boats and dirigibles from nearby Lakehurst Naval Air Station cruise close to the coast. Farther out, closer to the horizon, the big ships headed to or from the port of nearby New York City. The Atlantic Ocean became a companion and, in my imagination, a pathway to adventure and a bigger world.

WATER WINGS: 1950s

As I grew up in Lavallette, the beach became a recreational and social center. I can remember waiting impatiently for my parents to take us to the beach. They would spend hours watching as we showed off our improving swimming, diving, and wave-riding skills. My mother, a graceful swimmer, would help me develop more efficient strokes so I would have greater endurance and better breathing techniques. Unless the water was unusually warm, my father would do little more than let the expiring waves encircle and bury his feet.

There were mornings our entire family would go to the beach hours before the lifeguards set up their stands. We'd take our two water spaniels and delight in swimming with them, and then head back to the house, ravenous for breakfast.

Each summer, friends from the previous year returned, and we would form clusters of towels on the beach, waiting for the tides to change and bring in riding waves. Then we would transform into communities of inflatable rafts at the perimeter of breaking waves.

One of the great moments of my life—perhaps when I was about ten years old—was when my parents agreed that I had enough aquatic knowledge and safety skills to go swimming at our beach by myself. It was the equivalent of giving me keys to the family car: I had freedom and could spend unlimited hours in and below the water.

In time, I became a strong ocean swimmer and an accomplished body surfer. When I was 15, I began preparing for what was, for me, the the crowning achievement for an ocean swimmer: to become a lifeguard.

I began to swim greater distances and completed junior and senior lifeguard courses. I learned rescue techniques, how to block and parry a grasping drowning victim, and how to administer basic first aid.

I was about 22 here, in 1969, fresh out of college and loving my lifeguarding life. I spent about a decade guarding beaches in New Jersey and Florida.

The day after I graduated from high school, I competed in a lifeguard test for one of the spots on the Lavallette Beach Patrol. It involved timed races on the soft beach sand, swimming in the frigid waters of early June to "victims" with a line and taking a surfboat out

Lifeguards with the Lavallette Beach Patrol trained and worked extensively with sturdy surfboats just like this one.

through the waves. Though nearly 30 competed for the 10 new spots on the squad, I managed to win one of the coveted openings. It was a gateway to responsibility, development of a deeper understanding of the ocean's actions, refinement of observation skills, unknown prestige and visibility, and a whole new social life.

It was probably at this point that I began to develop the distorted confidence that grew into hubris that would lead to the deepening and humbling circumstances I found in Cuba.

SEA LEGS & STUDIES: 1960s

I continued to lifeguard between college semesters and for two summers after graduation. The sunny days were filled with conversations with lifeguard bench partners, rescue drills, rowing surfboats, riding surfboards, helping an occasional lost child, or administering minor first aid for cut toes and splinters. Actual rescues were a rarity, in part because I had learned to be proactive, preventing serious problems before they developed.

I studied Architecture Design in a five-year curriculum at Clemson University in South Carolina. By my junior year, my GPA had been pulled down by a year of low grades in physics and three semesters of calculus. Ahead was statistics, an academic career-breaker. If I didn't raise my grades, I would be forced to drop out altogether and face the draft for the increasingly unpopular Vietnam War. By now, veterans were returning from combat zones in Asia and revealing the distortions and lies that routinely were broadcast by the military and those at high levels of the U.S. government. Reports of corrupt South Vietnamese leaders also were circulated. This was even before Richard

Nixon made the election-year claim that he had a "secret plan" to end the war.

If I left college, I was convinced I would be sucked into the vortex of combat. I shared the perception of many that it was a civil war in which we did not belong and could not win. Already, friends and classmates had died there. The U.S. role seemed increasingly meaningless as the death toll grew and one crooked regime after another assumed power in South Vietnam.

I began to consider changing my major to English, with no clear career goal other than to become a teacher or write for a newspaper or magazine.

My grades gradually improved by cutting back on my involvement in my fraternity, rarely dating, quitting extracurricular activities like rugby, and concentrating on getting high grades in reading and writing classes.

During winter and semester breaks, I put in a few days working on my brother-in-law's clam boat, more for the experience of being at sea beyond the sight of land than to make money. I learned a little about throwing spring lines, working a deck winch and helping with dry dock repairs. Occasionally I would offload clumps of bushel burlap bags of clams into tractor-trailers, which would take them to processing plants to be made into chowder.

I graduated with a degree in English and Fine Arts and looked for a decent job, but I was coming up empty. I could find menial work, but it lacked engaging challenges. Bartending, lifeguarding and working as a film production assistant were fun—and included an active social life—but barely provided for necessities or a sense of career building. My mind felt like a fish out of water, gasping for air; it was atrophying slowly, day by day. I was looking for insight and a larger view of the world; to see rarely seen and exotic places, to meet people from other cultures, to discover deeper meanings, to make some kind of a difference for mankind. These were all strong desires—stronger than the need for stability and security.

Shortly after graduating, I obtained a Merchant Marine card, enabling me to sign on to an ocean-going freighter. The prospect of long voyages, devoid of female relationships—and the approaching summer—made me reconsider. But the lure of the sea would call again and put me in the predicament I could not have foreseen.

JE DOS: JUNE 2, 1973

We stayed in the Cuban villa as prisoners for a week. Then we were told we were going to be taken to "another city for further processing." The tone sounded threatening, and it meant we were going to get farther away from our vessel and the water. Early the next morning—just before daybreak—an *aula* drove up: this was a jail on wheels, with four cells—two for two prisoners, and two larger ones crammed with 10 captives in each. As guards escorted us into the paddy wagon, I felt another burst of fear. In my mind, I saw a taunting face saying: "Now you're going to get it!"

We rode in that truck for 10 hours. Chet sat next to me in one cell with our backs to the driver's cab; Cal and Dan were in the other "first class" cell to our side. We couldn't see each other through the metal partition separating us. The heavy transmission droned on throughout the day, as Chet and I watched the other prisoners, all filthy from working on sugarcane farms.

As the truck rumbled on, we were hypnotized by the truck's rocking and its constant din. When not in a stupor ourselves, Chet and I kept an eye on our guards, checking their alertness to see if there were opportunities for us to speak. We spoke one or two times to each other, in soft tones, before the guards caught on. More than anything else, we tried to give each other moral support.

We stopped only once all day to stretch our legs and use the toilet at a rest area. We had only a tiny view out of the small side windows, so we quickly lost all sense of orientation in a land we had never visited, though we saw snatches of farmland. At one point, we could smell a fresh change in the air, just before glimpses to our left revealed the bright sheen of light careening off the south Cuban coastal waters. The turquoise Caribbean waters looked more inviting than any I had ever seen. We rode along the winding southern coastline for about an hour and then turned north, and inland.

Finally, near sunset, we arrived at what we later learned was G-2, Department of State Security—a small, beige three-story interrogation prison modeled after the KGB's Lubyanka Prison in Moscow. It had louvered openings, but no windows above the first floor. Set in a residential neighborhood on the outskirts of Havana, it was built in 1963 and was known as *Villa Marista.*

I was escorted to a small room, given an oversized tan jumpsuit and instructed to change into it. I was photographed and depersonalized with an assigned number. This was the beginning of stripping me—physically, emotionally and psychologically—of my identity. After my clothes, glasses, watch and boots were inventoried, a guard escorted me up two flights of stairs leading to a long, pale green corridor punctuated by a series of green doors. As he walked along with me, he whistled no particular tune. That seemed eerily familiar—as though I had somehow been here before. Later, I would recall why.

We stopped at the green door for cell number 14. It was made entirely of heavy gauge metal and—at eye level—had a little hinged door with a metal shutter so the guard could look in without opening the larger door. When it was closed, neither the guard nor the prisoner could see beyond it. I was ushered in without a word. The heavy metal door crashed shut behind me and the bolt slammed into place, jarring my bones. All freedom was gone. I was sealed in.

I surveyed my new concrete dwelling. My world was limited to just three and a half paces forward to a cold, grey wall. At the far end, light seeped in around inverted V-shaped louvered openings that ascended from shoulder level toward the roof and were constructed in such a way that there was no line of sight to the outside world.

This is my drawing of the cell in which I spent 30 days of solitary confinement. The fixed, louvered openings in the wall allowed in the colors of the setting sun and the sounds of Havana's streets.

I found this image online years later. What I had known as G-2, where I spent five weeks, was also called *Villa Marista,* and had underground torture chambers.

To my immediate left was a three-foot, square, partitioned space with a squat hole in the floor for human waste and s hower drainage; above my head was the end of a raw copper pipe that spouted water three times a day, serving as my drinking fountain and shower.

Beyond the "shower" hung two massive boards in steel frames suspended on one-inch chains bolted to the wall—bunk beds. Scratched in the heavy wood were the words "Bay of Pigs" and initials. Above the doorway I had just entered glass blocks and metal mesh sealed in lights that were constantly on.

This was my welcome to what I was to learn was Havana's notorious G-2, *Je Dos* in Spanish, pronounced "hay dos"—Hades in English.

Half an hour after I entered the cell, I was given a tray of greasy dinner: beans, some rice, and a yellow-brownish meat and grain concoction we later nicknamed puppy poo.

As the sun set, the light oozing through the louvers turned a light pink, and I knew my cell faced west and sunset had been taken from me. I could hear the sounds of a neighborhood getting quiet for the night—soft muttered greetings along the street, the motor of a passing car, mothers calling their children in from play.

Periodically, a guard would randomly open the small door in the larger cell door and look in. Satisfied I had not escaped or killed myself, he would then slam it shut, with a loud gnash of metal-on-metal that reverberated in the concrete cell. After it had been dark for about an hour, a guard brought a bag filled with *galletas*—large unsalted crackers. I took two bites and then fell into a troubled, exhausted sleep.

ALONE: JUNE 3, 1973

"*Desayuno!*"

I was awakened by the yell of the guard as he slammed the bolt of my cell open and then thrust a cup of coffee-flavored milk and a roll at me.

It was June 3, 1973, my first full day of solitary confinement. It was also my 26th birthday.

I had a life plan—and this was the year I would reach a milestone. When I was in college, after I left all aspirations of becoming an architect behind, I envisioned writing or directing films. For some reason, I had latched onto the notion that my "breakout" year would be when I was 26. It was a silly but strong concept. I thought I could make films to communicate universal messages and bring people of all cultures together. The great American expatriate director Stanley Kubrick was my idol. I believed cinema was the "New Literature"—bridging language and cultural barriers. Films could bring clarity to ideas and promote concepts of universal acceptance to wide audiences, promoting messages of understanding and tolerance.

Instead of such glory, I spent the entire day locked in a small space inside a locked building in an imprisoned country on a rogue island. Never had I felt so small or insignificant. My despair could hardly have been greater, yet, it got worse when I thought about my parents. They still did not know that I had even gotten on a boat in Jacksonville. They were expecting me to come home in a few weeks. Now they would worry about me. As far as we knew, no one but the Cubans knew what had happened to us. We were lost in the Bermuda Triangle.

Unbounded by the routines of time, chores or people, with little to distract or entertain me, I fell into a reverie. I would spend the entire day and into the night wondering: How did I get into such a predicament; where did this all begin; and how was I ever to get out?

I thought back to the events that had brought me to such lowly circumstances. The simple facts were that I was on a shrimp boat, we had navigation errors, a storm was approaching, and we were preoccupied with preparing for it. Although we entered Cuban waters with no ill will, we had military surplus, rafts, a small amount of SCUBA gear and weapons on board. Were we some clandestine paramilitary operation? Were we trying to whisk people out of Cuba? Were we CIA operatives?

No, in fact, I was a smuggler.

Actually, that's not entirely true. I was a would-be smuggler.

Although it wasn't exactly clear to me at the time, I also was a would-be writer looking for an experience to observe and record. My life had been mundane up to that point, or so it seemed, with only a few really vivid moments. I had had many gifts put before me. Like so many things that come easily, I took them largely for granted, though if anyone asked, I would have paid lip service to how good I had it.

My mother was tireless, raising her children compassionately and selflessly, and my father was congenial with a patient and an even-keeled disposition. Only once could I recall hearing him raise his voice with my mother—after she persisted in reminding him about some trivial task he must have seemed to have ignored. It only lasted a few seconds and then it was gone—either the issue was over, or they would continue the discussion later, outside of my presence. That was the way they were, and they were affectionate with one another in subtle ways. It was years later that I learned how uncommon such a harmonious relationship was. Every June they had two wedding anniversaries: one for the marriage they had kept secret when they eloped to Elkton, Maryland, and another marriage, almost a year later, when they could make it a public occasion.

There was little I lacked, and I was surrounded by relatives and supportive neighbors in a beautiful seashore resort community. Simply put, I had it good.

I'd had some adventures—hitchhiking hundreds of miles up and down the Eastern Seaboard while in college; a cross-country trip to Hawaii; living through earthquakes in California; and along the way, finding personable and intelligent female companions.

But I was looking for something more to satisfy my wanderlust. It came in July 1972 with a phone call from Chet, my friend and college apartment mate, who, after a pilgrimage to California and Mexico after college, had returned to live in his hometown of Jacksonville, Florida. We had sporadic contact over the years, and he was one of those people I never wanted to lose touch with.

"Hey, Gordy, what are you doing for the next few months?" I heard in his soft southern drawl.

"I don't have any big plans—got something in mind?"

"I've been working on a commercial boat, and I'd like you to come down here and help me out."

"As a deckhand?" I asked.

"No, actually, I'd like you to help me get the vessel shipshape and look after Mona while I'm at sea," he said. "You know how she is—kinda high-strung; she worries when I'm at sea, and kinda needs a babysitter. She likes you and I trust you to be discreet."

The previous spring I had traveled to South Carolina and Florida to visit Clemson classmates and Dr. Rex, my favorite professor, who had influenced me a great deal with his 20th Century Novel & Epic courses. I had met Mona on that trip, Chet's live-in girlfriend. A dark-skinned Italian beauty, she was struck by how similar Chet and I were in personality and demeanor. I didn't see it but took it as a compliment. I thought of Chet as a brother—a kindred spirit. He came into my life when I had become alienated from mainstream society during my junior year.

By my junior year of Architecture Design, I was averaging 15 or more all-nighters each semester just to keep up with elaborate design projects and my courses. There were times I fell asleep in classes, dragging my pen down my notepad—already filled with chicken scratch. Once I fell asleep in the middle of a physics quiz, waking up just in time to turn in my blank sheet of paper. Another time, I woke up in calculus class to see the entire room tilted and half the class staring at me: I had fallen asleep and started to lean over so far, the professor asked the other students to make sure I didn't hurt myself if I fell.

It was not going well. I needed to pick up my grades—fast. I began to take amphetamines to help stay awake during all-nighters, cramming for tests, reading 500-page novels or writing term papers. I had found the pills to be effective and they were commonplace among my classmates for the long nights of designing, reading, studying and writing. I saw the drug as vital for me to complete my assignments, to avoid the shame of total academic failure.

I needed something to take me out of the rut I was in. I had become disillusioned and felt emotionally isolated. I needed to collect myself, but I did not know how to do it. I was going around in circles in my head. When I really needed it, some new things came into my life.

This was during the late '60s when music, art, society, and politics were in a state of heightened agitation; when much of the country was polarized, and many people, particularly the college crowd, began to question on a large scale their lifestyles and the beliefs and convictions they had grown up with. The sweep of the late 1960s was a time of major upheaval, change and convergence accentuated by a series of assassinations—Malcolm X, Martin Luther King, Jr. and Bobby Kennedy. There were massive anti-war demonstrations and disrespect for elected officials and authority figures, and veterans returning from Vietnam were treated with scorn for contributing to a war that many felt was unjust—all against a backdrop of immense stadium rock and roll concerts, drugs, sex, and revolution in the air.

I began to associate with a band of college rebels and activists. Chet and I met casually through mutual friends around a coffee shop table during talks about the social issues that were on everyone's minds. He was a college junior, and I was a sophomore, and our acquaintance matured into a friendship during my junior year. Chet was charismatic, drawing flocks of people wherever he went, or so it seemed to me. It might have been his casual friendliness, his open and unpretentious manner, and his ability to laugh at himself as well as with others. His influence was positive during a time of great personal need.

Chet's manner, idealism, and kindness reminded me more of the person I used to be and wanted to be again.

Soon I began to visit Chet's other friends at the Clayburn House. Nowhere did the rebellion of the era seem stronger at Clemson than at the off-campus Clayburn House. Most of the students living in its warren of apartments were architecture students, former architecture students, and intellectuals who had a strong creative or offbeat flair. They were adventurous and unconventional. They built their own furniture and hanging beds, stuck up backlight posters, and were on to the most avant-garde happenings. On my first visit at the beginning of sophomore year, I heard the precedent-setting *Revolver* album by the Beatles issuing from one of the apartments. Later, time at the Clayburn House would be marked by listening to *Sgt. Pepper's Lonely Hearts Club Band* and *The White Album* for the first time. The evolution of the Beatles and their music seemed to propel our own transformations.

I ended up moving into the rambling Clayburn House shared by Chet and a close circle of his friends—most of whom I knew casually already.

A few days after the move Chet was checking my attitude about marijuana. "Have you ever tried pot?" he asked.

"No."

"Would you like to?"

I had read about it—after all, you had to live in a cave not to have heard of the rise in its use, along with the advent of readily available

I drew this image of Chet months after I returned to New Jersey. His idealism, demeanor and kindness were positive influences on me during some tough days in college.

amphetamines. Based on all the sources I read, marijuana was not addictive, had no established negative side effects, and had been used throughout history.

"Sure," I replied.

"Well, we'll probably have some this week . . . and don't worry, I'll try to make sure you have a good trip."

It was clear he approached marijuana as if it were a sacrament, a substance to provide insight and harmony.

That Friday, Chet invited me to the apartment he shared with Gopher, a former Architecture student turned Psychology major.

We gathered around the ground floor apartment that overlooked the rim of the black water in the swimming pool. It had been neglected for so long it was filled with years of dead leaves.

We were sitting on low couches and Gopher rolled a joint, lit it, inhaled deeply and passed it to Chet who took a drag and handed it to me.

"Here, Gordy, inhale and hold it," Chet said. "Sometimes the first time, people don't get off on it."

I inhaled the smoke, held it for about 10 seconds, and handed the joint back to Gopher. In a few minutes, my body seemed to have loosened up—that I was lighter than before. I started to notice all kinds of ironies in our warm friendship, of communion with one another, of a bond with new subtlety, delicacy and richness in the music. My mind seemed to skip and romp through thoughts and concepts.

After about half an hour of light chatter and lots of laughter, we went into the kitchen and played "Mystery Food." We would take turns keeping our eyes shut while someone gave us something to eat. Not knowing what to expect heightened our senses of taste, touch and smell. Someone popped a chocolate-covered cherry into my mouth, and it exploded with a variety of flavors and textures.

Chet paid close attention to see how I was handling this new, altered state. He served as a guide and treated pot with the respect many had for the far more potent LSD. Once he was convinced I was handling it well, he left me to my own devices but would check up on me from time to time, adding reassurance to a profoundly new experience.

For me, pot was preferable to alcohol, which made me feel dull and oafish—like a Neanderthal. Mornings after drinking, it was easy to say to myself, "I'm not going to do that again." Pot was the clear winner.

The students in the Clayburn House ended up living semi-communally and developed bonds that lasted for decades. Chet, more than anyone else, helped bring us all together. On the weekends, we would have small parties in several apartments at one time. People would wander from one to another, crashing on couches and mattresses on the floor to the sounds of the Animals' *Sky Pilot, Time* by the Chambers Brothers, *The Who Sell Out*, Iron Butterfly, Country Joe and the Fish, Buffalo Springfield, Traffic, Cream, and the Beatles.

Chet graduated first. He taught for a while—more to avoid the draft than to make a living. He lived with a former Clemson coed—something that was culturally unacceptable and almost unthinkable at that time. It also created friction with his parents. When his extended affair ended, Chet moved to the West Coast.

My change to major in English with a Fine Arts minor worked: in only a year and a half from the beginning of my junior year, I got high enough grades to graduate in December of 1969. Just two months before graduation, a draft lottery had been held to determine who would face compulsory military service in response to the inequities of the current system. My birthdate had drawn No. 306 in the lottery and I knew that I was not likely to get drafted.

I graduated a year after Chet and took more courses to get teacher certification. We kept in touch sporadically, but two years later, our paths would cross and lead to major decisions.

CRUCIAL DECISIONS

It wasn't until springtime two years later that I traveled to South Carolina to see former classmates and to Jacksonville, Florida, to see Chet and meet his girlfriend, Mona.

We visited for three days, and Chet showed me around the Jacksonville Beach area, where he was working as a mechanic. I felt accepted by their community of friends and even got along with Chet's sometimes-ferocious German shepherd-husky, Boss. Mona treated me like a Chet clone and enjoyed the attention of someone similar to Chet in appearance and behavior.

During the following July, Chet called to say there were delicate matters he didn't want to discuss over the phone. He mentioned it would have something to do with me leaving my home in New Jersey, and he wanted to know if I would be willing and able to do so. Rather mysteriously, he asked if it was okay to send Mona up to visit me for a few days, and she would fill me in on the details.

Two weeks later, I picked Mona up at the airport, and she told me what Chet had been talking about: he was helping to outfit a small freighter to be used in a marijuana smuggling operation.

When it had been restored to seaworthiness, he would be the vessel's mechanic. They planned to take it to Jamaica to get thousands of pounds of marijuana, and he wanted me to be his man on the ground in Jacksonville to look after Mona while he was gone. Knowing Chet, I also knew he was counting on me to look after her if anything bad happened to him.

Mona stayed a few days. During that time, she said she had told Chet that she was attracted to me. He told her he thought of me as a brother and had no problem with her sleeping with me. Comments from Chet over the phone supported that belief.

Looking back, it's hard to imagine the context that made all that seem so easy to accept. It was part of the 1960s evolving sensibilities. We aspired to a more communal way of living, of sharing resources, ideals, information, pleasures and emotions. The idea of sharing a girlfriend seemed more like a bond, even an act of sharing among friends. If everyone was consenting and the relationships were good, what could be wrong with it?

On the other hand, I wasn't much interested in a physical relationship with Mona. She was a little too high-strung and impulsive and required high maintenance. She had low self-esteem and needed constant reassurance and affection.

Besides, I had my own girlfriend, Lorna. My relationship with her had started innocently at a party more than a year earlier in northern New Jersey.

There were few people I knew at the party, and most were heavy drinkers or couples. I began to think making the drive there was a mistake. While most of the partygoers were getting outlandishly drunk or were in their own tight cliques, I sat on a hallway couch to figure out whether to stay a little longer or leave. Lorna walked by and said hello, which led us to comment on the intensity of the drinking and this sprouted into a conversation. She had lovely strawberry blonde hair and a freckled sweetness that made her seem younger than her 21 years. We ended up on the couch, away from the action and became acquainted over the next hour.

We talked about whom we knew in common, where we lived, what we did for a living and how we spent our spare time. I told her about my recent return from a three-month stay in Hawaii and an even longer one in Los Angeles. Lorna told me she was with friends who were renting a summer cottage only a dozen blocks away from where I lived in Lavallette.

At some point, we kissed. After a few minutes, she told me she was a virgin. I thought this was to discourage unwanted advances or assumptions on my part. I told her I understood and respected her restraint, but I misunderstood her intentions. She said that she did not want to be one any longer.

"Don't worry," I replied. "Someday the right person will come along, and you'll know that's the way it was intended to be."

"That's what I mean—I believe you're that person," she said.

The statement was so bold and unexpected that I was jolted into speechlessness for a few moments. After I recovered, my first reaction was to dismiss it as a curious "in the moment" statement—perhaps she was kidding, yet part of me believed she wasn't. I looked into her eyes and saw only determination. How do you respond to such a statement?

"Are you playing with me?" I asked.

With conviction, she told me she was serious.

The whole notion of her being so deliberate and straightforward with a newly met person filled me with a giddy mix of shock, bewilderment, adventure and inflated ego. Once I recovered, I wanted to reject the notion, but not her. She was desirable but seemed too innocent and delicate. The difference in our age was only a few years, but it seemed greater. A year earlier I had a charmed summer job that seemed to provide the right conditions for several women to fall into my lap. I fell for one of them and followed her to Honolulu, where she was a University of Hawaii student. After a few months, though, the affair ended unhappily, and I returned to live with a college roommate who had moved to Los Angeles. Only a few months later I was back on the East Coast and engaged in this conversation with Lorna.

"I'm honored by the offer," I told Lorna, "but I don't want to be a part of this. You are a lovely person, but I don't feel a strong romantic connection and I don't want you to either."

"Don't worry, I won't," she replied.

Before we parted, she invited me to a party at her rental in Lavallette. In the coming weeks, we saw each other at barbeques and parties. We talked a lot and developed what I thought of as a casual bond, but I wanted to stay at arm's length.

Sometimes Lorna would bring up the subject of initiating her to sex. She made it sound as if it was a barrier to experiencing the great unknown and the richness of life. My resolve weakened; in a matter of a few weeks, that barrier was removed.

We continued to see each other over the summer on the weekends she came down with her friends. It was an affectionate relationship that continued but became less and less frequent, in part due to the 60 miles between our homes. Throughout the fall and winter, I worked at the docks in Point Pleasant, New Jersey, taught as a substitute, and found short-term menial jobs. There was little time to make the journey to northern New Jersey to visit Lorna.

By springtime, our relationship felt as though it had run its course, and I tried to withdraw from it altogether. I didn't want to hurt her feelings because I still liked her, but that was as far as I could see the relationship going.

That's when I contacted Chet to revive our friendship, get a fresh perspective and put some distance between Lorna and me, and that's when the seeds were planted that led to Chet asking me to help him a few months later.

When I returned, Lorna was trying to keep me as her boyfriend; at that point in my life—a little more than two years out of college—

I was barely able to commit more than a week. Besides, Lorna's behavior had become disturbing, and I didn't know how to handle it and be sensitive to her feelings. I had been let down hard myself and knew how bad it felt. But Lorna's persistence and will were formidable. She knew how to play on my sympathies.

I had started to date Maureen, a friend's sister, and Lorna sensed that my interest was waning or spied on me. On my birthday, late at night and unannounced, she showed up at my house with Band-Aids on her wrists. They could not have been more glaring.

"What's that all about?" I asked her.

"I just wanted to see what it would be like. They really aren't deep," she said, trying to downplay the Band-Aids. She told me she just felt bad, but it seemed to be directly linked to our withering relationship.

It made me feel guilty for not having the emotional connection she wanted. The result was that I said goodbye to Maureen and stayed with Lorna out of a sense of obligation, not knowing how to ease out of the relationship without causing serious harm. When the second opportunity to go to Florida and stay at Chet's arose late in the summer, it seemed like a way to run away from some of my problems. I thought an "out of sight, out of mind" situation would make me unavailable to Lorna and her interest would fade.

After Mona returned to Jacksonville, the idea of moving to Florida, at least for a few weeks, seemed like a good idea. Chet said I could live with him and Mona, and they'd share food costs with me. Money wouldn't be a big problem—Chet could provide me with a small salary for my help with projects and errands. I had gotten along well with Mona and the idea of a change of scene offered advantages, among them was the appeal of spending the fall in Florida.

I had told Mona to tell Chet I would give serious consideration to his proposal. There were only a few weeks of summer left, and he didn't need my reply for a few days.

There was another thing that compelled me to leave home—at least a little. My mother had had a stroke two years earlier. With great concentration and determination, she could walk, but she had lost the use of her right arm. She was very proud and refused to use a wheelchair except to move around her workspace. Perhaps worst was the emotional effect the stroke had on her. Part of it was her frustration with what formerly had been simple tasks—dressing, writing, moving small items—but now, she would have crying fits. At times it seemed there was nothing we could do or say to ease her distress. These breakdowns could occur at any time. Sometimes it was when other people were counting on me to fulfill a responsibility. The dilemma was whether to stay and try to console her or walk out when she seemed so needy. This sense of helplessness made the idea of traveling south—essentially of running away from a problem—seem more like an adventure each day. I could get away—from the routine, from Lorna, and from the helplessness I felt around my mother.

As I weighed the merits of going versus staying, the trip south seemed to be a good fit. It might open up job possibilities in Florida; perhaps I could rise out of the rut I had fallen into. Life felt like it had a lackluster, I'm-not-making-progress, bland routine.

I talked myself into going, believing that I wouldn't be gone too long. There would be a sense of exploration and the opportunity to meet new people, to learn new things. During my earlier visit, I met several of Chet's friends. Who could guess what might lie ahead?

By mid-September, I had committed to go south. I loaded up my black VW bug and headed for the interstate, feeling free of the bonds of responsibility, stopping off to visit a former girlfriend in Columbus, South Carolina. I had hoped to have an epiphany—perhaps some resolution. All that seemed 2,000 light years away now.

BIRTHDAY REVERIE: JUNE 3, 1973

I could hear the clatter of metal trays as lunch was brought to each cell. I could tell that most of the cells on my floor were empty because I only heard three doors open and close before they came to mine. The guard thrust a spoon and an aluminum tray containing some kind of jelly, plain rice with a few beans and a roll into my hands. I ate in silence and continued thinking about the events leading up to this situation.

While in Jacksonville Beach, I had slept on the couch in the small bungalow that Chet and Mona rented. The first night, Chet brought me up to speed on the details of his project. He had been outfitting a small boat to transport marijuana from the Caribbean and offload it to fast boats off the coast of Florida. I arrived just after the financial backer and organizer for the venture had been swindled out of the vessel he had paid for. To keep his name off incriminating documents, he had the vessel registered in someone else's name. The guy with his name on the documents had legal title and took off with the vessel, selling it to someone else and pocketing the money, reportedly in New Orleans. Obviously, there were thieves in the den and trust was a fundamental issue.

Another vessel had been purchased, but it was in bad condition. It was a 65-foot shrimp boat that needed engine work and maintenance on its machinery with a hull in need of caulking and paint. Chet also tried to find isolated spots where the contraband could be offloaded discreetly and then distributed. I went with him several times to scout locations within 50 miles of Jacksonville.

Eventually, Chet became involved in parts of the project that were confidential and that he could not disclose, even to Mona or me. It looked as though, instead of a visit lasting weeks, it would take longer than expected. I was becoming a burden on Chet's finances, so by Thanksgiving it became clear I would need to get my own source of income. One of Chet's friends had become a manager at the Bluffs Point Club and through him I learned of a nighttime bartending opening. Then, another one of Chet's friends, a VW mechanic named Sheridan, offered me a job helping him rebuild engines during the day, almost as often as I would like. I would earn $25 for each engine he repaired and reassembled. Occasionally we would get as many as three engines and restore them in less than five hours. Sheridan would wax profound about engines and women he had met, all the time with one hand on a power impact wrench and the other often hoisting a vodka martini.

Finally, Chet told me that the smuggling operation was in place. I was to take good care of Mona while he was gone and see that she stayed glued together. It was just a few weeks before Christmas, and he expected to be gone for about 10 days. We had no communication with him after he left. Each night, Mona would get anxious about the dangers Chet might be confronting, and to calm down, she would take sopers, pills similar to Quaaludes. The sopers induced a mild sense of drunkenness, loss of inhibitions and sleepiness—all in about 45 minutes. Each night he was away, I would watch as she nearly toppled over into an ashtray from the sopers. I would try to get her into bed before she became a lifeless form on the couch.

Finally, after more than a week, we got a call from Chet. The obvious dangers were over, and it was a jubilant reunion. He confided to me later that he had been paid $25,000. One of his first purchases was a large red Craftsman tool chest on wheels. After a few weeks and a few fine dinners, Chet told me he and Mona were going to get married and needed time alone.

Chet had a small trailer on his property, so I moved in for a few days. He had bought the trailer in California years before at an auction of confiscated vehicles. For less than $200 he had picked it up with a '47 Dodge. Despite being more than 20 years old, Chet marveled that the Dodge dashboard clock still worked. He had lived in the trailer when he went to Mexico for several weeks, brought it all the way cross-country and then left it parked in his driveway for years.

I stayed there for a few weeks, then found an affordable one-room apartment. It was a lonely life I was leading. My only real friend there was Chet who was going through some kind of self-examination and working on his relationship with Mona; he just wasn't available at the time, and I respected that.

By late winter, work with Sheridan had gotten sparse, just at the time that the Bluffs Point Club needed a pool and beach lifeguard, so I began working there during the day as a lifeguard and at nights as a bartender. I was earning decent money with no time or place to spend it, although I had a few after-work drinks with Becky, the attractive 40-year-old receptionist at the club's front desk who had flirted with me for months. She was 15 years older than me and we came from different worlds, but we were both lonely. She had come to my bed two evenings after we had had drinks, but there was no glue to the relationship—we both just wanted someone to hold and physical comfort.

Things were going well, but it wasn't much better than the rut I had been in New Jersey. I was unhappy and alone when not at work.

Weeks went by without any contact with Chet, and we seemed to be in different orbits. Then I got an invitation to Chet and Mona's wedding in February.

It was a "hippie-style" wedding—colorful faux formal clothes for the bride and groom with an outdoor ceremony and reception. I took photos and was happy for them, if not a little apprehensive about their future.

A week later, Chet came over and asked me if I'd like to go on a voyage. He explained that Tom, the skipper on the previous smuggling run, a former U.S. Army helicopter pilot who had served in Vietnam, had left the country after their successful voyage to Jamaica and Chet had been promoted to skipper. Two crewmen were being assigned to him, but he needed a crewman he could trust, who had experience, would be discreet and could help him get the vessel in better working order. It needed provisions, fittings, caulking, paint and parts. He also wanted me to be a backup navigator.

"Gordy, the waters are crystal clear, and you can see 30 feet underwater," Chet said. "We can dive at atolls along the way."

The last time I had been in waters like that was in Hanauma Bay in Hawaii, one of the most stunningly beautiful places I'd ever seen. The bay was formed eons ago when the side of a volcano had eroded and been flooded by the Pacific. Over the millennia, it had become a canyon of coral, filled with exotic fish of brilliant green, blue, yellow, and red, and had been made into a preserve for aquatic life. The prospect of seeing such natural beauty was beguiling.

I was also tempted by the mystery and possibility of seeing the rare phenomenon of a "flash of green." This occurs when the sun sets during certain atmospheric conditions when the diminishing light curves around the horizon and the sky acquires only the green hue of the spectrum for moments. I would travel through phosphorous-rich seas, glowing at the bow and in the wake. Flying fish would skim the waters for hundreds of feet like heralds of our progress.

This voyage would be an adventure that would close the book on what had been a lonely and unmemorable chapter of my life. I had no real women friends and life had lost a lot of its luster. It was far less than the expectations I had had nine months earlier before leaving New Jersey. And it would end the chapter with Chet on a positive and unifying note. It would make me rich in adventure, and it would fuel my pen as a hopeful, but unaccomplished, writer.

I told him I'd need a few days to think it over.

"Okay, Gordy, but I'll need to know by the end of the week."

Then he added, "I'd really like to have you on board. I need someone I can trust."

The most compelling reason not to go had to do with my parents and was driven home during a phone call from my father in mid-April. After the first few words, I sensed that there was something important on his mind, so there was little of the usual small talk.

"Hi, Gord, how are you?" he asked.

"I'm fine—what's happening at home?"

"Well, it sounds as if you don't have any promising work going on down in Florida, and I could sure use your help," he replied. I heard the urgency in his voice.

"I was thinking of coming home, but a little bit later, perhaps in early June," I said.

"Between my work and evening meetings for the Borough, getting the rental units ready for the summer, and looking after your mother, I've got my hands full. And your sisters are tied up with their kids."

My father wasn't complaining, but I could sense his distress. He was now 62 and the simple things he did as a younger man were becoming more difficult. And I felt he missed being with me, his son, something that I would not fully appreciate until I had my own child.

He went on to tell me that, since her stroke, my mother had sharp mood swings, and was frustrated with the effects of the stroke. My father spoke to me more like a friend and confidant.

As I had moved through college, our relationship had changed, and I was engaging with him more as an adult. I began to understand and appreciate who he was and why others respected him so much. In turn, he realized that I was trying to move out into the world, first by my trip to California and Hawaii, now this journey to Florida, which had lasted nearly six months with little to show for it.

My dad rarely asked me for help, so I tried to put him at ease. "Dad, I'll plan to be home in a few weeks."

"I'd appreciate that, son. Let me know when you're getting ready to get up here."

"Okay, Dad, I will. Take care and give my love to everyone."

"I will. Goodbye."

That my dad asked me to help him now was significant. My conscience was not loud enough to make the unselfish decision and step back from my commitment to Chet, however.

Up to this point, I had a clean slate. I knew going with Chet could have grave consequences. But I thought it would be an opportunity to establish myself as a journalist without a publication or sponsor, a chance to establish myself as a writer with an unusual experience and perspective, and an opportunity to go to sea again and explore exotic waters. I was already getting ready to leave Florida, so it fit well with the flow of changes.

My thirst for excitement and to see the Caribbean, along with a sense of camaraderie and loyalty to Chet, outweighed all the lessons my mother had taught me. The subjective reasons to go became more compelling: I'd get to see the Bahamas and be at sea for a week or two with Chet, one of my closest friends.

I thought that if everything went well, I could be home in less than three weeks with a great adventure to relay. I was torn.

A few days later Chet asked, "Are you in?" I said, "Yes."

I had stopped working for Sheridan altogether, then I gave notice to the Bluffs Point Club. During the first two weeks in May, I became

Chet's gofer, buying maps, mariner's almanacs, tools, fittings, flashlights, batteries and storage cases during the day.

At night, I immersed myself in how to navigate by "shooting the sun" with a sextant, a timepiece, and the study of the intricacies of celestial navigation.

Now I had all the time in the world, in this tiny cell, away from all that was familiar and dear to me. I could only look inward and feel that my life was a series of blunders and bad decisions that seemed to mock me in my despair. I was a prodigal son.

I had no timepiece, no sky, no stars, and no horizon. I was lost.

SOLITARY: JUNE 3–5, 1973

That day I prayed, cried like a motherless child, and tried to find a way to cope with these dire circumstances. I began to obsess with regret over all the failures that had led to this point in my life. To try to stem the despair that felt so overwhelming, I spent the day trying to recall all the happy birthdays that had come before.

I tried to think of a way to improve my outlook. I recalled Dalton Trumbo's *Johnny Got His Gun*—a book that had left a strong impression on me. It told the story of a World War I soldier waking up in a hospital after he was wounded. The entire book is an interior monologue of the soldier as he returns to consciousness and describes his thoughts as he tried to assess the severity of his injuries. First, he realized he couldn't see. He consoled himself by thinking it might be only temporary blindness, or perhaps his sight was blocked by the bandages he could feel around his head. The soldier thought of how he could learn to cope with this new limitation. Once he had made his peace with that blow, he realized he was missing a leg.

"Okay,"he thought,"I can learn to adapt and walk with a cane."

But then he realized he did not have the other leg either. He thought of all the things he did with his legs—playfully chasing his brother, jumping into the water, kicking a can. His self-revelations continued. He had no arms and would not even be able to shoo away the fly that crawled across his bandage. And most of his face had been blown off. He could not even speak. He thought of all the things he wanted to say—of how he would never be able to hug the members of his family or his girlfriend.

These reflections gave me a new perspective on my circumstances. I was still in one piece and could hold on to the hopes of being with my family once again. That was how one man's misery lifted another out of the pit of despair.

I thought of the most wonderful present I could give myself. I imagined the sweetest experience possible and embellished it, down to fine details. My eight-year-old niece, Kirstin, was the personification of sweetness and innocence. I had always felt a mystical connection with her and her mother, my oldest sister.

Shortly before I moved to Florida, Kirstin had begun piano lessons. There in this lonely concrete cell, divorced from all human warmth and daylight, with no certainties whether I would be there a day, a week, months or years, I imagined Kirstin at the keyboard, playing Beethoven's *Fur Elise,* one of my favorite piano pieces. The image of her playing this sweet and simple melody helped transport me away from my fears, regrets and sadness. As I pictured her dress, the light falling upon her, the clarity of the notes, and the remarkable exchanges between human spirits, I felt terribly alone.

The day seemed interminable, interrupted only by a lunch of beans and watery soup and the water spigot coming on for five-minute intervals three times that day. I took a soapless shower to rinse off the perspiration and then air-dried.

Finally, the light coming through the louvers began to turn pink. I imagined the beautiful sunset I was missing, how many I had ignored before, and the night sky with all its constellations that barely got a glance in my busy life. I longed for the most commonplace experiences and felt hopeless.

After dark, the guard brought his nightly bag of stale *galletas,* slamming my cell door with a bone-jarring jolt on the way out.

I wished I could sleep as much as possible to make the time more tolerable, but sleep didn't come easily, and without the exertions of a normal day, I probably slept even less.

The next morning, as I listened to guards escorting a couple of prisoners, I realized why so many things seemed strange, yet eerily familiar. I had read part of Alexander Solzhenitsyn's *The First Circle* a year earlier. It had been a gift from Carol, a precocious college coed I had met when I was lifeguarding. She was a blue-eyed brunette, a Spanish-Irish beauty, and we would sit in the sand by the lifeguard stand at the end of the day and discuss books, music and films. Despite the gulf in our ages—she was six years my junior—she was quick-witted and cosmopolitan, yet innocent. Our discussions were a stew of free-association banter. We'd laugh at our wordplay, comment on the news from near and far and the marvels of life. On this day, I found myself connected to Carol through the book she had loaned me.

Now, I found myself walking through Solzhenitsyn's description of being inducted into Lubyanka, the oppressive interrogation prison in Moscow. The real similarity hit me when I heard the guards escort anyone through the stairs and halls and whistle the entire time they were escorting a prisoner. In Lubyanka, Solzhenitsyn said, the guards clicked their tongues on the roof of their mouth when they had someone in escort. This was done to alert any other guards to keep their prisoners out of sight—in a closet, vacant cell or facing the wall. No prisoner was to have any knowledge—even sight—of another prisoner. The entire place was designed to break people down, to ensure their loneliness, isolation, desolation and dependence. They were to see only authority figures.

Shortly after I awoke, I recalled that Solzhenitsyn was not seen by prison officials and was not given such basic items as a toothbrush or soap until he had been alone for three days in his cell. This was part of the process of breaking people down—making the prisoner obligated to his keeper. That thought cooled my heels a little, and gave me a slight edge in understanding the process I was being subjected to and how deliberately it was designed.

Sure enough, on the third day, shortly after breakfast, a guard brought me an inferior quality Chinese toothbrush, toothpaste that tasted faintly like licorice, soap and a towel. I brushed my teeth three times.

Later in the morning, a guard opened my door and motioned that he would escort me down the hall. We passed several green cell doors and then turned left down the dark and narrow stairs at the end of the hall. The guard whistled as we walked but said nothing. We came to a small room and the escort recited a litany in Spanish that sounded something like, "Private Fernando delivering prisoner 256 as ordered. *Venceremos y viva Fidel!*" Captain Rodriguez, a thickset man in military dress, sat behind the desk, motioned for me to sit and discharged the guard with a salute.

He had a broad face, thick neck, black curly hair and dark eyes. From his demeanor, I sensed he was a mid-level officer. He spoke broken English with a heavy accent and asked basic background questions: Where I was born? What was my address? He was cordial, but businesslike, as he took notes. He offered me a cigarette, which I accepted. It was my first in more than a week.

Rodriguez began asking about my employment and military records. I told him I had worked at a country club shortly before going to work on the *Silver Sands,* which he found more interesting than I thought it warranted. And he seemed to find the fact that I had not served in the U.S. military even more significant—that it was an important piece of a mosaic he was constructing. He then began questioning me about my background as a navigator. He wanted to know how we could depart from a U.S. port without special clearance and how we could have gotten guns if we had not been working for the government. Rodriguez seemed to have no idea of the freedoms of American society.

He then said the Zodiac raft on our vessel was identical to the ones used by the CIA in their frequent raids on the Cuban coastline. I told him I did not know the U.S. was conducting attacks on Cuba. He thought I was lying.

Next, he discussed the other members of the crew and my relationship with them. He asked their ages, occupations and how I knew them. I explained that Chet was the only one I knew, having roomed with him in college. He then asked if I thought the crew might have had an alternate purpose. This shocked me, as I hadn't even thought of such a possibility. He tried to undermine my confidence in the purpose of our cruise.

The methodical questioning—interrogation seems too harsh a word—lasted for nearly two hours; prolonged by occasions when we had language difficulties. I would use some slang or his thick Spanish accent would require repetitions. As Rodriguez walked me to the guard post up the hall from his office, he asked if I had received the dental hygiene items and towel he had ordered for me and if so, did they meet with my satisfaction.

Then he asked if I would like something to read.

"Certainly," I said. I was so hungry for something to exercise my brain that I would have gladly read an insurance policy—repeatedly! He also said he would send me cigarettes.

Returning to my cell, I resumed my perch on the bed and thought about the interview. I could not figure out the meaning behind several of his questions. Months later their direction would become clearer.

Shortly after lunch, a guard brought me cigarettes, matches and the English edition of *Granma*, the official newspaper of Cuba. It gave a hostile view of the Monroe Doctrine, implying that it was intended to keep European interests in the New World from creating a foothold so the U.S.A. could have it all to itself. This was a general edition about colonialism and how the United States had imperialistic designs on the entire Western Hemisphere in the early 19th century. The edition had articles that traced U.S. imperialism all the way back to Thomas Jefferson. The newspaper also talked of the brave martyrs of Cuba's history, particularly *José Martí*.

My brain sucked up the material like a dry sponge. I spent the remainder of the day wondering about our conversation and reading the newspaper. It seemed curious that every time Richard Nixon's name was mentioned, the "x" was replaced with a swastika.

I had not had a cigarette since we had gotten off our boat and hadn't noticed the withdrawal. Now I seized the cigarettes and savored each smoke even though a few puffs made me dizzy. Although the package said they were *suave*—meaning mild—they tasted more like a cigar, had paper filters and were so potent that I smoked just three, even though they provided a break in the monotony of the day.

As the first week of solitary confinement wore on, the fear that I would be held for a prolonged period weighed on me heavily, and I feared either or both of my parents would die during my absence. My mother had had the stroke, and my dad was a lifelong Old Gold smoker. Would we have no moments of closure on all the things one wants to say to those they love when the link of time and space is about to be forever broken?

My father was always looking out for us. After I got low midterm grades during my first semester of college, he drove 750 miles from New Jersey to South Carolina to make sure I was all right. The fact is, he was worried for me—was my state of mind okay? And probably—I would understand in later years—he missed me, his only son. Then, after a meeting with the head of architecture studies, and a meal with me, he completed the 1,500-mile round trip home.

Mother was a tireless worker, often holding two jobs, but she always had time to listen and talk to us. When I was in the third or fourth grade, I came home from school with a couple of my friends with the notion we would publish a local paper. My mother embraced the idea, helping us figure out what we wanted to report on and dividing up the labor of selling ads and subscriptions, writing articles and interviewing people in town. Within a week or two, we had collected enough articles and she typed up five copies for us to take around door-to-door to enlist subscriptions. Since we didn't have a press or mimeograph, we would charge people $.02 to read it and decide if they wanted a subscription. In our little seasonal resort town, the novelty of a newspaper published by 10-year-old boys was a welcome diversion during the off-season.

I was one of five intrepid 4th graders who started a monthly newspaper in Lavallette, named appropriately, *The Junior Press.* We lasted about four years. I wish I still had a few copies. (left to right) Joe Wutka, Sandy Zabrowski, Jimmy Boekholt, Jr., Gordon (standing), and Steve Anteau.

We got enough advance subscriptions that my mother fronted us the money for an inexpensive mimeograph. She also wrote to popular 1950s television shows like *Strike It Rich, I've Got a Secret,* and *What's My Line?* to see if they might like to have us on as guests. To our amazement, *Strike It Rich* said yes, and four of us got an early start on our 15 minutes of fame. We ended up winning $105 because of our crusade, which simply involved donating a part of our income to a charity like the March of Dimes. Through a "Heartline" call, we also were awarded a beautiful Gestetner mimeograph that seemed like the Rolls Royce of duplication machines in the late 1950s.

The little newspaper lasted four years until the novelty and interest were worn down by what seemed like an additional homework assignment.

◈ ◈ ◈

Each day in prison I reflected on my life, which felt like a succession of numerous blunders.

Screw-ups in baseball and football games weighed on me. My experiences were in contrast with the accomplishments of my father, an exceptional athlete by all accounts. I'm sure he hoped I would surpass his achievements. Though I tried, I didn't come close to being on the state championship baseball and basketball teams he played on, or to his success as an undefeated pitcher at Lehigh University.

Then there was my social life. Girls and women I had liked, and who, often unbeknownst to me, had liked me as well, seemed like so many opportunities for an enjoyable social life that had slipped through my fingers. All too often, I would find out their attraction to me was beyond anything imaginable. What I wouldn't have given to have just a few minutes to talk to Carol H. from my Lavallette Grammar School?

Then I began to wonder: Where was the moment I had taken the wrong step? When had I started on the course that led me to this lonely and forgotten cell?

AT HOME

Perhaps if I had known of the ongoing news reports and communications while we were in solitary confinement, I might have felt more at peace and not so alone and forgotten. Almost from the moment I was put in solitary, what we thought was our private enterprise became news in Florida newspapers. The accounts mentioned that the Swiss Embassy was serving as an intermediary since the U.S. did not have direct diplomatic relations with Cuba. The reports, which were filled with inaccuracies, must have scared our families.

The Journal, Tuesday, June 5, 1973

Jacksonville Shrimper Missing Off Bahamas

A search of the ocean in the vicinity of the Bahamas was begun today by the owner of a Jacksonville-based shrimp boat four days overdue on a trip to Grand Cayman Island.

Chief Engineman G.N. Millhof, duty officer at the Mayport Coast Guard station, said no radio communication has been received from the 65-foot *Silver Sands* since the vessel left Mayport May 23.

Luke Bing of Jacksonville, the vessel's owner, said plans called for the shrimp boat to return here on June 1.

Aboard the *Silver Sands* are Ashley Longstreet, the master, Dan Halford, Calvin Giron and Gordon Hesse. Bing said the course planned by Longstreet would have taken them close to the eastern tip of Cuba when the vessel traversed the passage between the Bahamas and the island.

He said the trip was intended as a break-in run for a new engine, which had been installed recently. "The hull was in good shape and mechanically, the whole vessel was in good shape," Bing said.

The owner said he has chartered a twin-engine plane which was to leave Miami early today to begin searching the Bahamas area.

There was a successive exchange of information and telegraphs between Chet's mother, with the U.S. Coast Guard and the State Department as the mystery began to unfold to our families.

Western Union Telegram

June 7, 1973

To MS. LILY LONGSTREET AND SISTER MARY ADMINSTRATOR ST FRANCIS MEDICAL CENTER 1803 BARRS ST JACKSONVILLE FLA

HAVE RECEIVED RESPONSE FROM LT MILL, MIAMI COAST GUARD HE INDICATES THAT COAST GUARD HAS LAUNCHED FULL INVESTIGATION INCLUDING RECONNAISANCE FLIGHTS FOR LOST BOAT SILVER SANDS. WILL RELAY ANY ADDITIONAL INFORMATION IMMEDIATELY UPON RECEIPT. BEST REGARDS.

CHARLES E BENNETT MC

At this point, our families were praying that our vessel had not been sunk or that we had not been lost at sea. Their fears eased when more information came out, but it was just the beginning of a new nightmare. News reports continued to be printed and telegrams sent, as we sat in our cells, unaware of the growing publicity.

Times-Union, Sunday, June 10, 1973

Mayport-Based Shrimp Boat Shows Up in Cuba; Had Been Reported Missing

The Mayport-based shrimp boat *Silver Sands,* missing since June 1, has been located in Nuevitas, Cuba, according to a Coast Guard spokesman.

According to the spokesman, the vessel was on a trial engine run to the Grand Cayman Island. The Coast Guard was checking with fish camps and marinas along the coast when it was notified to conclude its search because the vessel had been found.

A check with the Miami Coast Guard revealed that the 65-foot shrimp boat had been in Cuba since June 6. The information, however, came to the Coast Guard from the State Department and "We really don't know anything about their situation except that," said the Miami spokesman.

"Any more information would have to come through the State Department. They get all their information from the Swiss Embassy down there (in Cuba). There'll be nothing over the weekend. We were just advised to discontinue our search," said the spokesman.

The *Silver Sands,* owned by Luke Bing of Jacksonville, left Mayport on May 23. It was due back June 1.

Bing said the course planned by the ship's captain, Ashley Longstreet, would have taken them close to the eastern tip of Cuba when the vessel would traverse the passage between the Bahamas and the island country.

The trip was designed as a break-in run for the new engine installed in the craft, Bing said.

Western Union Telegram

June 11, 1973

To MS. A. D. LONGSTREET JACKSONVILLE, FLORIDA

THANKS YOUR TELEGRAM. HAVE IMMEDIATELY CONTACTED STATE DEPARTMENT AND WILL RELAY ANY INFORMATION IMMEDIATELY UPON RECEIPT. BEST REGARDS,

CHARLES E BENNETT MC

The Journal, Tuesday, June 12, 1973

Shrimp Boat Carried Guns?

The Cuban government claims it found guns, radios, lifeboats and thousands of dollars aboard an American shrimp boat it captured early this month says Sen. Lawton Chiles, D., Fla.

Chiles said Saturday the Swiss embassy notified the State Department that the Cuban government considers the items suspicious and has been questioning the four-man crew of the shrimper *Silver Sands,* which is based in Jacksonville.

Chiles said the State Department questions the report from Cuban police of "tens of thousands of dollars on board the vessel."

Families of the crew say the men had about $1,000 with them to pay expenses during the cruise to the Cayman Islands to test a new engine.

Chiles said the items the Cuban government labeled suspicious included a rifle, 45-caliber pistols and two radios.

He said the Cuban government contends the rubber life rafts are the same type Cubans use to escape the island.

The boat's owner, Luke Bing of Jacksonville, said the rubber rafts were aboard the vessel as lifesaving equipment.

Bing said the radios were the normal type used by vessels operating off the coast.

The Swiss embassy has been negotiating for the release of the shrimp boat and its crew: Captain Ashley Longstreet, 28, and Gordon Hesse, 28, both of Jacksonville, and University of Florida students Dan Halford, 24, and Calvin Giron, 25.

The boat left its home base at Mayport near Jacksonville on May 23 and was to return on June 2. The Coast Guard searched for the missing vessel until June 8 when the Cuban government announced it had captured the 65-foot boat.

Chiles said that the Cuban government has not said whether the boat was captured within its territorial waters.

GENESIS: JUNE 1973

Where did this story begin?

Oddly enough, it may have been the first time I got drunk.

I was at a small party, probably when I was 19, and there were five guys and three girls at a friend of a friend's summer beach home while the parents were away, and I was feeling left out. I got the idea that a few drinks would make me feel better. When the room started swirling, I went off to a private porch, gulping air like a fish out of water, trying to get myself back to a stable state. In the background, I could hear the conversation as the guys plied the inexperienced girls with drinks.

"I had four beers tonight," said one of the girls, boastfully drunk.

"That beats the old record of three and a half," jeered one of the sager predatory males.

It was then, while I lay on a wicker porch couch, that all the advertising images of alcohol showed themselves to be false. You know—the sophisticated man with impeccable hair, flinty gaze and a smile that oozed power while he casually nestled his drink—a glass of Scotch on the rocks—in his left hand while his right rested on the tiller of a spacious sailboat. Hanging onto his shoulder was a vibrant beauty with long tresses. Shimmering water flowed in the background. There was a romantic sunset, just as the lights were coming on. Or maybe they had martinis, goblets of red wine or snifters of cognac.

These images had nothing to do with the state I was in as I stumbled down the wooden porch steps to retch on the ground.

In that moment, I kept thinking, this is what all the fuss is about? That's it? I feel like crap. I can't walk in a straight line, my vision is skewed, and I feel worse than when I had the flu. There has got to be something better. Ultimately, it turned out to be marijuana, which led me to Cuba.

Flash forward two more years from my drunken realization: I'm in college in the late 1960s. I've learned to hold my beer—even to enjoy it to a certain degree. I'm in a fraternity and playing rugby, mainly to go to the beer parties afterward, sing bawdy songs and share the arm-over-shoulder brotherhood of body collisions, mud, and competition. I know my limits and I'm getting on okay, but the liquid doesn't do much except limber me up a little, cutting the edge of the anxiety of academic overload and the tension of sexual longing. There had to be something better.

The easiest way for me to rack up better grades was to take courses in my strength areas: those that required reading and writing abilities. My grades were barely above water—too low to transfer, so I became an English major. All of a sudden, college wasn't the grind it had been with design projects that involved inked boards, models, contour maps, juried presentations and weeks with just a few hours of sleep each night. I got my degree, with more credits in my minor, Fine Arts, than in my major, English.

I came back to New Jersey and worked on the clam boats. On evenings when the bounty was good, we would throw enough bushel burlap bags of clams to fill up three tractor-trailers. I also worked for a friend in his commercial filmmaking and animation business and began to substitute teach. When summer rolled around again, I was drawn back into lifeguarding. But something had changed. I was 24 and most of the guards were three or four years younger. I felt more isolated. I took a job guarding and bartending at the Surf Club—a nightclub where scandalous casual affairs with a stream of changing partners were typical for the bartenders, bouncers and musicians. It seemed everyone was out for a last-chance romance or something to fill the time.

During the day I would lifeguard, and on the weekends I learned how to bartend. On the weekday evenings, I would date. Life became a blur of lovely 20-something women, each a unique adventure. Most were little more than five-night stands.

Now in a windowless cell, with no one to talk to, that seemed like ancient history.

LECTURES: JUNE 17, 1973

After two weeks of solitary confinement, I was summoned from my cell, taken down the flight of stairs and down a hall, away from the corridor of cells. I was brought back into the small room with no windows. Rodriguez told me he wanted to go over a few details with me. He asked me a few questions about our vessel, how well I knew the skipper, and a few more.

Then the part I was half expecting: "Do you know what Socialism is?" he asked.

Instantly, a tawdry vision of myself in a grainy black and white video played in my head as I imagined being paraded before movie and television cameras: the despicable capitalistic and imperialist drug smuggler. I imagined how they would try to break me down and make me renounce my country—the country that was fighting Communism in Vietnam, the country of Watergate and Richard Nixon. In my mind, I already began to feel the rack of the inquisition.

"Sure, I think I know what Socialism is, but I bet you have a better explanation," I replied. I sensed that Rodriguez was waiting for that cue.

"Socialism is de way to Communism," he began in rather bad English. "Under Socialism, everyone works for everyone. De peeple work in de factories and make de shoes. And de shoes are for everyone."

So far, this didn't seem too bad. He went on and seemed to make some sense. This sure beat sitting in the cell and feeling lousy all day long. Then he seemed to veer off.

". . . and de people make de loaves, and de loaves are for everybody. De loaves are for de rich people and de poor."

The images of people hospitably breaking bread didn't seem to fit with what he was saying.

"And when people break de loaves, they go to the court. Then they must face de judge because of de loaves."

He went on for at least 15 minutes trying to explain "de loaves." I couldn't figure out what he was saying or why people would go to court for breaking bread.

Then I remembered that the Spanish alphabet had no "w." He had been talking about the "laws."

With that realization, I felt a sense of great peace—my brain hadn't rotted due to my isolation. He made sense after all. The people make the laws, and the laws are for everybody.

Rodriguez told me he would send some things to my cell.

In a few days, I was called out from my cell again and again met with the interrogator.

He was cordial and asked if I had received the items he had sent. I said yes and commented that I appreciated the newspaper. Aside from craving reading material, I figured he might as well think I was sympathetic to his point of view. He told me he would send something else to read that I would probably find interesting.

He then presented several badly typed papers with a "confession." It said that we were smugglers planning to obtain drugs in Jamaica when we were intercepted in Cuban waters. It detailed our two firearms, rafts and walkie-talkies. There seemed to be no point in not signing it: They could hold us in their prison forever. No one knew where we were, and the U.S. did not have diplomatic relations with Cuba.

Then, as I was being ushered out of his office, he asked if the cigarettes were to my liking. I told him they were strong, and he said he would send some that were more *suave*.

The next day I was given a fresh pack of *Liqueros*—milder cigarettes with filters made from rolled paper. I was also given an English translation of *Che Guevara's Diary of the Revolution*. The book about Castro's revolutionary comrade and fighter was a valued gift. I threw myself into reading it as slowly as possible. After nearly a week, I had read it three times. The first time I read the 150-page book to see what happened. What was the story? The second time I read it for character development. The third time I read it for all the secondary characters. The one who interested me the most was not Fidel, Raul, or even Che—who I always felt was the most striking of the pack—but Camilo Cienfuegos. A Cuban by birth, Cienfuegos had been working as a busboy in San Francisco when Fidel's uprising began. He returned home to carry on the revolution. Che cited Camilo's courage under fire and, despite a peasant's upbringing, his skills as a leader in some of the most daring fighting. Within a year of Castro's takeover on January 1, 1959, Camilio reportedly flew from Camaguey to Havana, but he never arrived, and no plane crash was ever found. In effect, he went up and did not come down. Some were suspicious that he was too popular and a threat to Fidel's newly claimed power and may have paid the ultimate price.

I spent the next day killing time by trying to remember the lyrics to my favorite songs. I discovered if I concentrated, I could recall most of them, all except *Lucy in the Sky with Diamonds* from the Beatles' *Sergeant Pepper's Lonely Hearts Club Band*. Although I had heard it hundreds of times, I could not remember whole blocks of lyrics. The songs of Joni Mitchell, the Doobie Brothers and Simon and Garfunkel played in my head with greater clarity as my isolation grew longer.

DREAMS & VISIONS: JUNE 24–30, 1973

Then I began to notice a curious thing each morning. When I awoke I could recall, almost in their entirety, the three dreams I had each night. Without any pressing daily business or chores in my little cell, I could devote my thoughts to remembering the dreams. It seemed each day I was going deeper into myself—exploring people, events and unacknowledged feelings from when I was little more than a toddler, a young boy, a young man. It was as though I could put my life up on a pedestal and observe it from new sides and insights.

One night, after three weeks in the cell by myself, I dreamed I was with my father, and he offered me a taste of his black-and-white malt milkshake—one made with vanilla ice cream and chocolate syrup, our favorite drink. In the dream, I had a taste of the drink. I could feel the cold, coarse chocolate milk flavor on my tongue with the distinct finish of the malt as it slid down my throat. It was bliss. Then I began to wake up. It was the middle of the night.

No! I thought, *take me back to my dream—I don't want to wake up to a living nightmare!*

I tried to get back to sleep so I could have *just one more sip!*

It was not to be.

I longed for that taste and spent hours thinking about it before I fell asleep again. One night, after four weeks alone in my cell, I had a vivid and strange dream.

I was at a place along the edge of the ocean. The buildings all around were derelict. Concrete had crumbled or been shattered and fallen into the waves that lapped against concrete walls. Metal reinforcing bars protruded through the broken chunks of cement as the waves receded from the wall. It was unlike any place I had ever been, and I couldn't imagine where the strong images had come from.

The next morning, I was summoned from my cell again and taken to the interrogator.

He was brief. We were going to be set free.

He looked for my reaction, but my emotions had been suppressed for so long that my reaction was flat—bordering on complete disbelief. Perhaps it was a cruel joke that I could not entertain. But as it turned out, it was real—sort of.

He said our clothes would be arriving shortly. My disconnect was nearly complete.

Instead of jumping for joy, I felt empty.

I was escorted back to my cell. Then, as sunset approached, I was summoned again.

The next part was a blur. Clothes were issued, and I was reunited with the other members of the crew. We looked at each other and laughed nervously. We had all grown beards during our captivity. But we hesitated to speak for fear we would say something that might make the guards change their minds.

IMMIGRATION BUILDING: JULY 1, 1973

We waited in the receiving area of G-2 until dark when two Fiats with Ministry of the Interior insignias drove up. We carried our sea bags out to the vehicles and handed them to soldiers who put them in the trunk. We rode with two of us crammed in the back with a soldier. It was dark and raining lightly as we drove at breakneck pace through the Havana streets. The air and the sights were seen through new eyes, eyes that had been starved for color, action, perspective itself; the tires sizzled musically on the damp pavement; the air held bouquets of aromas; the few lights of the city reflected off the roads and splattered colors on the windshield of the car before the wipers made them splatter anew. We traveled for 15 minutes and were taken to a mansion called the Immigration Building.

We walked up six steps to a small stone porch and then through a foyer and past two bored and sleepy looking men lounging in front of a television in a great room. Our army-fatigued chauffeurs led the way, carrying our sea bags. The contents were emptied out and inventoried in our presence as we tried to figure out what kind of place we were in. The mansion had marble floors, 14-foot-high, coffered ceilings and a

This sketch shows the Immigration Building, a three-story mansion with an ocean-fed pool on the waterfront, where we stayed twice—first when we were told we would be freed, then after more than seven months in prison.

majestic 6-foot-wide sculpted staircase. Either it was deserted, or the other residents were sleeping.

Here the change in our treatment was easily discernible. We were offered the Cuban version of limeade: half a lime squeezed in a glass with sugar added. We were asked if we'd like a snack before going to our sleeping quarters. We were offered bread, butter, jelly and a coarse, dry and salty cheese. We learned later that the cheese had been extended with potatoes.

We were also told not to leave the premises. In effect, we were on house arrest.

Dan, who was always quick to strike up a conversation, spoke to one of the men who was not preoccupied with the evening's TV program and found out that the men housed there were seamen who had either changed ships in Havana, been injured and unable to complete their voyage, or were no longer needed on their vessel and were awaiting a flight or ship to their home port. They were from Pakistan, Greece, Italy, Spain and Yugoslavia.

While the other bags were being inventoried, Chet told me what he had learned at G-2. He said he had asked Rodriguez if our country had been notified by the Cubans of the seizure of our boat. Rodriguez told him that the U.S. State Department had inquired about us, and the Cuban government had acknowledged that we were being held indefinitely. This reassured us—now five weeks since our vessel had been boarded—that at least our families knew we were alive and also that the Cubans could not be entirely irresponsible in their treatment of us.

By the time we had eaten and our belongings inventoried, most of the seamen had gone to bed. It was suggested to us that we do likewise, though we were pumped up with excitement at having left G-2 behind. Freedom might be right around the corner! We went up the large curving staircase, passing stained glass windows and were shown to a room with four beds. None of us could sleep. We talked about our impressions, hopes and fears as we chain-smoked cigarettes.

At one point Cal wandered around the dark building, returning a few minutes later to report that we were located within a hundred feet of the ocean. We followed him to a porch and observed the sea through the darkness. In our excitement, we ended up staying awake most of the night.

At dawn, Chet and I were up before Cal and Dan. We went downstairs as the other residents of the building—soldiers and transients—arose. Chet and I walked out to the area behind the Immigration Building as one of the seamen from Italy worked out with a barbell set that was there for the guards. The sun was bright, and the July air was already warm but cooled when the breeze blew off the water.

Between the building and the seaside-facing side of the building, 25 feet from the rear steps, was a concrete swimming pool that was fed ocean water through two large openings over which a walkway passed. In the water were big chunks of concrete with reinforcing rods protruding through the surface.

"Chet," I said, "this is the place I saw in my dream two nights ago."

All the distinctive images were there, as if my dream foretold where I would be. It was just one more eerie element to a weird dream.

We began to discuss the problems we might anticipate with the *Silver Sands* when we returned to her. Chet thought the batteries might easily have gone dead as some of the systems may have been left on.

We were interrupted by a call to breakfast: eggs, coffee-flavored milk and bread.

This gave us an opportunity to observe the seamen who were lodged in the building. For the most part, they were a friendly lot, and acquaintances were made quickly, though sometimes the conversations got confusing. One involved a question I spoke in labored Spanish to a seaman who spoke French as a second language, to one of the other residents who spoke Arabic, but knew French. Sometimes the information and ideas got mangled, but fortunately most of the seamen spoke fairly good English. They provided us with insight into everyday life in Havana, as we were not permitted on the streets.

Although most of the seamen who came to the Immigration Building stayed no longer than one week, two teenagers from Morocco and Algeria had been at the building more than three months. Their names were Omar and Gela—we began to call them Hockeypuck and Hog. They had been stowaways on ships, and no one wanted to claim their citizenship, so they were in limbo.

Hockeypuck looked like he had been hit in the back of the head by a puck in such a fashion that his teeth splayed out; he reminded me of something from a Daffy Duck cartoon. Hog, on the other hand, ate with such gusto and pace that his nickname was easy to establish. He ate food as though his hands were shovels and his mouth was the furnace. The pair also filched a few of our personal items.

Shortly after breakfast, we met Garcia, the director of the Immigration Building, or at least that's how we perceived him. He was a short man—perhaps 5 feet, 6 inches tall. He smoked the largest cigars and they seemed to accentuate his shortness. He reminded me of a young George Burns.

In the coming days, he replied with an indefinite answer to almost every question we asked.

"Could we contact our families back at home?"

"The Minister of Immigration first needs to review your case."

"Do you know how long that will take?"

"Not long," he replied.

The days at Immigration slowly melted into one another as our restlessness grew. We spent our days playing chess, listening to the Watergate hearings on a portable radio, sunning, and reading any books we could get our hands on, though most were in Spanish.

Most nights, television would provide pre-Revolution movies in English with Spanish subtitles. Later it was indisputable that many of these films were selected for their "sociological" content and for their depiction of a slice of "typical" American decadence. Probably these distorted views helped many Cubans believe they had a better way of life. Most of the films starred Humphrey Bogart, James Cagney, George Raft or Edward G. Robinson in gangster roles. *Who's Afraid of Virginia Woolf* was considered to be a glimpse into the domestic scenes of a typical American marriage. It was shown with surprising frequency.

By now, after two weeks in our new residence, we renewed our questions to Garcia about when we would be allowed to leave. His comments were perfunctory—mere lip service: "We can tell you nothing until the Minister of Immigration has reviewed your case." He and other representatives used the expression "soon" frequently and casually.

The soldiers posted at the Immigration Building served in a number of roles. Some were cooks, some administrators and still others alternated on guard duty at the front entrance to the building. For the most part, the atmosphere was cordial, although a few of the soldiers were less than amiable. Cal, with his constant requests, often tried their patience to the limit. Julio was one of the friendlier soldiers who served in an administrative capacity. His love of contemporary English and American music immediately gave us something in common. Late in the evening he would put on his transistor radio and listen to the U.S. music stations, frequently naming the artists of songs and other numbers they had recorded. He did this with great pride and satisfaction.

On nights when there was spare food in the kitchen, he would bring it out for us. In the evenings, Dan would talk to Julio in a friendly way. The guard believed Communism was the best political and economic system, but he had almost no knowledge of other models and much of what he did know came through the filtering of Fidel Castro's functionaries. The conversations were true dialogues, and despite different points of view, they were cordial and respectful.

We also struck up a friendship with Saleem, a Pakistani seaman. He was recovering from hepatitis and had to wait until his blood count had reached a certain level before he could leave. He had a permit to go out on the streets of Havana, and he would return with tales of the conditions he witnessed. Cuba's economic standards were far worse than any of us had estimated. He told us of having been invited to the home of a Cuban family, and he noted that the portions of meat were very small and that he got the largest of these small pieces. After the meal, he learned that the family's entire allotment of meat for the week had been used up that night. He said the food we were being served at Immigration—the food we all grumbled about—was far superior to the food the average Cuban ate. He described how a young woman had approached him one night during a street festival. She would go to bed with him, she said, for the envelope of fine stationary that protruded from his pocket.

Frequently we would see sailors leave the building with conspicuous bulges in their waistbands; later we learned that these were nylons and panties, which were worth valuable favors.

One day, we were surprised when Chet received a letter from his wife. In it, she explained how, when she had been questioned, she told authorities that we were delivering the vessel to Grand Cayman Island where it would be used for a salvage operation. This information would end up being crucial to our circumstances, and gave us the notion that if we did get to our vessel again, we could continue an altered version of our plans.

After we had been at Immigration for two weeks, a seaman who was headed to Spain the next morning volunteered to smuggle out a letter for us. He identified with the treatment we had received from the Cubans and wanted to do whatever he could to make things easier for us. We hastily composed a short letter explaining that we were okay, but did not know what the Cubans intended to do with us as no one seemed to be giving us a straight answer. When he left early the next morning, we gave him the letter and our thanks.

Each clear day, which was almost every day, I would look out over the ocean and see the high cloud formations to the north caused by the thermals over the Florida Keys—just 90 miles away. Chet began to join me at sunset on the seawall, which bounded the rear area of the Immigration grounds. This became a silent ritual for us as we longingly looked toward the Keys and watched the clouds above them turn to explosive orange and subside into soft shades of purple before they were consumed in darkness. As the stars began to poke out, I searched for the constellations I had become familiar with more than two months earlier. It was comforting to watch the trajectory of the Big Dipper pointing to the north, Cygnus the swan, Leo the lion, and my astrological constellation, Gemini, the twins.

One day we were told that a representative of the Ministry of Immigration was coming. When he arrived, early in the morning, Chet approached him and asked for something definite on when we were leaving. He replied that our case was unique and very complicated. He promised to let us know the moment he found out anything.

Our earlier enthusiasm and initial belief we were going to be set free was beginning to wane. We began to recognize that our house arrest was more significant than we first thought. We became more desperate; when another seaman heard of our story and offered to smuggle another letter out, we decided to go ahead with it. This particular seaman said he had been shot in Red China by Communists and even showed us the bullet hole in his leg as if we doubted that it could have happened. He was more vocal in his disapproval of the Communists. Something did not sit well with me about him, however. The others wrote a letter and gave it to him. He, too, left early in the morning. The letter never reached its destination. Later we decided he was planted there to get information about us.

It was now approaching July 26, the anniversary of Fidel Castro's first ill-fated attempt to inspire the Cuban people in opposition to dictator Fulgencio Batista. For the three days preceding the 26th, Havana was turned into a carnival. Each night the television would show tall floats decked with dancers pulsating to the Latin and African rhythms. To my eyes, it seemed like a badly cast and gaudy pagan ritual that reminded me of the sacrificial rites on the island of King Kong. During the day, parades of military hardware with jets flying overhead were telecast. It appeared to be something like our Fourth of July but with the emphasis on military might and orgiastic dancing.

Finally, late in the afternoon on July 29, we received the word we had been waiting for: pack your things and get ready. After the initial exuberance, I had reservations. We had had no warning that we were to be moved. My doubts exploded when Chet and I went to the seawall to talk about this abrupt notice and watch the sunset. When we drifted close to the perimeter of the Immigration grounds, one of the guards told us to come closer to the building. We saw armed guards on top of the building where we hadn't seen them before.

This all seemed out of place. We had been led to believe we were going home. As we waited inside with our sea bags, our tensions began to build. Our hopes were dashed when our transportation arrived—it was another *aula!* My heart clenched like a fist. We would not be going home "soon"—if ever.

G-2 REVISITED: JULY 29, 1973

As the vehicle picked up speed, each of us was lost in our private thoughts.

Wondering where we were going preoccupied us as we began to pick out one or two familiar landmarks. We traveled through Havana, then out into the residential area that radiated from the center of the city. As the van slowed down and turned two tight corners, we realized we were returning to G-2.

There was very little "procedure" this time. We were directed, one by one, upstairs to the room where we had exchanged our civilian clothes for the tan jumpsuits two months earlier. We figured more solitary confinement was in store. Dan and Cal went ahead of me. I went next, leaving Chet behind. As a guard escorted me down the familiar corridor flanked by green cell doors, I wondered how long I could hold out.

When we stopped at one of the doors, I expected to see an empty cell. When the cell door opened I was jolted. Inside were Cal and Dan. It was so unexpected that my fears momentarily left me. The anxiety had been so great, I could not help but laugh. Dan and Cal grinned back. Somehow this strange reunion brought us an odd joy.

The company was sure to make this indefinite stay more palatable, despite the cramped quarters. Within a few minutes, the same surprised scene was replayed when Chet's face appeared at the entrance to our cell. Like me, he was stunned to see the cell was full.

This cell was larger than the previous one and had four bunks. Cal and Dan got the two on top that hung on opposite walls. Chet and I got the lower berths. The aisle between the pallets was less than 14 inches, but we suffered it tolerably well with our time spent on the top bunks except when it was time to sleep.

That first evening, we tried to figure out what was going on and why. We began delving into everything different officials had said. We contrived all kinds of explanations and interpretations to every subtle nuance, to all the phrases we had heard, and speculated dozens of scenarios. We still found it impossible to believe that lying was a function of the Cuban bureaucracy. All the talk got us nowhere—the situation was incomprehensible.

No one was summoned from the cell for a week. We had no soap, no toothbrushes and no cigarettes. Exercise was all but out of the question as we only had about 12 square feet of unoccupied floor space. During daylight hours, we perched on the top two pallets and talked and talked and talked. I began to envy Cal's ability to sleep as much as 20 hours a day.

Often, like foxhole buddies under fire, we would talk of the bash we would have when this whole incredible mess had been straightened out. When topics began running thin, we got caught in the futile exercise of discussing veal, London broil, lobster, red snapper, and fresh fruit. The arrival of bean soup, rice, rice pudding, and stale *galletas* snapped our minds back to reality.

By the fourth day of confinement, we had all become a little wacky. Cal had discarded his jumpsuit. Dan would rap on the cell door and try to bum cigarettes from the guards. They ignored him. Strangely, he had developed a taste for *galletas* and frequently asked for seconds.

When he requested them—possibly more out of astonishment than for any other reason—they obliged him with handfuls of the bland crackers. Somehow he managed to keep a sense of humor. To a certain point, it was infectious, and we somehow managed to avoid being absorbed into the bleak vortex.

Finally, on our seventh day in G-2, Chet was called out. While he was gone, we speculated wildly about what might be happening. He returned within an hour, and we pelted him with questions. Rodriguez had just told him we were going on trial. When Chet asked what the charges were, Rodriguez had been vague. He told Chet that the worst we could get, by his estimates, was a few weeks on a "work ranch." He dismissed Chet's further questions, telling him that we would be provided a defense counsel, as the Cuban courts would never permit someone to be tried without the aid of counsel. Rodriguez gave him no further details but did say we would be moved soon.

An hour later, before we could speculate much further, we were all called from the cell. We changed back to our civilian clothes and waited in the entrance area of G-2 for transportation. When another *aula* pulled up, we were locked inside.

This time, it seemed different: The guards who rode in our section of the wagon seemed sharper: they were a little steelier and alert than any we had seen during our time in Cuba. And their uniforms were pressed. Chet, a gun aficionado, noted that they carried AK-47 automatic weapons. It appeared that we were now greater security risks and a crack detail had been assigned to us.

We traveled 25 minutes through the outskirts of Havana, through shopping areas to warehouse and industrial areas, and through a tunnel that went under the harbor. We emerged on a steeply inclined highway and, as the *aula's* engine ground through the low gears, I caught a whiff of the ocean. As we moved further into more pastoral areas, we followed a smaller road that was flanked by trees. We were moving into a deserted area. This did not feel good. The *aula* braked to a stop, and we were told to get out. There were no buildings in sight. We were in the country. The soldiers motioned us up a hill to a tree line.

Each of us tried to come to a conclusion other than the one that seemed obvious: We were about to be executed. Every molecule of my body tensed in terror as we approached the summit, and the soldiers followed with their weapons at the ready.

The moist, soft wind blew eerily through the trees. Every moment was etched in sensual detail—the blended aromas of earth, grass and plants. The breeze was gentle and mild on the face, neck and arms, and I became conscious of its weight and humidity. Life and its elements seemed magnified and rich with definition. I could hear sounds that were always there but never noticed—our breathing, the footfalls of booted feet. The leaves made soft music as they brushed against one another. The color of the sky, the subtle play of light on the trees and the clouds' shadows slipping over the grass took on ethereal life.

It appeared there was to be no trial after all. Soon there would be no fear—time was about to end. I thought of the family I loved and would never see again. Each of us silently expected to be gunned down in the next few moments. The seconds stretched out; time had become elastic. And then a tranquil acceptance came over me: I would die here in a forgotten and anonymous hillside. There would be no witnesses. My family and friends would not know where I had come to an end. There would be no last appeals, no final messages for loved ones. I prepared to cross over to another realm.

We continued walking and after several hundred yards, we could see over the peak of the hill. Parapets suddenly came into view as we rounded the summit. Then, behind a cluster of trees, I spotted a drawbridge. The 40-foot walls descended into a dry moat. Finally, we saw a citadel—an immense walled city. I felt a weird elation—we were not going to be shot, only imprisoned.

As the adrenaline began to subside, a new fear took hold as I realized we would not be seeing this place if we were not here for the long haul.

LA CABAÑA: AUGUST 9, 1973

As we walked over the drawbridge, we got a good look at the 3-story deep moat. The face of the walls had 10-foot-high openings on each side of the entrance with grates at regular intervals. Hanging out of these openings were clotheslines draped with faded towels, shirts, pants, blankets and underwear.

Passing through the main gate, I realized the significance of the word *citadel*. We were in a walled city with narrow cobblestone roads, fronted by walls that were broken up into quartermaster shops, rooms with piles of blue prison uniforms, a barbershop, administrative offices and storage rooms. Had it not been for an occasional passing jeep and the soldiers' garb, I would have felt transported back more than two centuries.

Our walk turned into a hike, then we entered a subdivision of the fortress and were led to a holding cell. The four of us spent the next four hours in a windowless and moldy vaulted chamber that could have accommodated dozens more people. During this time, several military personnel passed, occasionally stopping to look in at the strange, bearded Americans. For the first time, I felt like a caged animal in a zoo.

Every so often I would try to find out more about our situation, but limited Spanish vocabulary usually caused the Cubans to laugh rather than answer. Obviously, they were accustomed to prisoners who pleaded their innocence.

Adjacent to our cell was another holding cell. We were astonished to hear a voice from that cell ask, in precise English, if we were Americans. We said yes and were asked why we were there, which raised our suspicions. Chet asked the unseen speaker what he was doing here.

"I am a prisoner," he replied. "I object to the government and am therefore considered a criminal. I have learned to speak English during my years in prison."

Chet asked about the prison.

"You are in *La Cabaña*—a fortress, military outpost and prison," he said.

I shivered when I heard the name *La Cabaña*. I recalled seeing documentary films of the executions authorized by Che Guevara that had taken place at *La Cabaña* in 1959, soon after Fidel Castro had assumed power. Formally known as *Fortaleza de San Carlos de la Cabaña,* the fortress was built by King Carlos III of Spain to protect the harbor after British forces briefly captured and held Havana. It was the largest colonial military installation in the New World when it was completed in 1774, taking 11 years to build. For 200 years, it had served as a military base and a prison. Originally, it could accommodate about 6,000 people and resist a blockade for more than a year. It was long thought, at least by the Spaniards, to be the strongest fortress in the Americas and protected the largest city in the West Indies.

Immediately adjacent to *La Cabaña* was *Castillo de los Tres Reyes Magos del Morro,* commonly referred to as *El Morro*. Construction on it began in 1588 and continued until 1630. In 1845, a tower almost 100 feet tall was added and outfitted as a lighthouse. It is a distinctive hallmark of the entrance of Havana's harbor.

The voice from the other side of the wall continued to ask questions, but we were so paranoid about speaking to the unseen voice that our replies were vague. We all were worried about him being a plant—a jailhouse snitch—to get information from us when our guard was down. How strange to finally meet up with a sympathetic voice, but to be so suspicious.

Finally, we were led to a quartermaster's storage room where the shelves were filled with piles of blue denim clothing, sheets and boxes of soap. We became upset at this point when we were each issued two shirts, two pairs of pants, a pair of sneakers, a sheet, and two different bars of soap—one for bathing, the other for laundry. We tried to refuse these items, trying to communicate to the quartermaster that a mistake had been made, and we were going to trial, not to prison. We had no idea whether he understood a word we said, but he became increasingly gruff and insisted we change into the issued clothing while he stored our possessions. Seeing no other alternative, we relented and changed into the coarse, cheap and unfamiliar clothing.

We returned to the holding cell and spent an uncomfortable night trying to sleep on the stone floor. In the morning, Chet and Dan were led out. Within 45 minutes they returned, with short haircuts and clean-shaven faces. Without his mustache, Dan reminded me of my father. Chet's transformation was even more striking. He was almost unrecognizable with short hair, and he was beardless for the first time in years.

Cal and I were led out, down a complex maze of alleyways, to a barbershop, complete with barbers' chairs. As I sat down for my first haircut in four months, I noticed a man in a blue denim prison uniform sitting in one of the waiting chairs along with a few other observers. He had a strikingly American demeanor and appearance. With his chiseled look, he reminded me of a Clint Eastwood character, and when he spoke, he had a midwestern drawl that marked him as undeniably American. He asked us who we were and how we came to be there. Cal, always blunt and quick to speak, told him that our boat accidentally entered Cuban waters and asked the guy his name.

"I'm Tex," he replied, but he denied he was an American and stated he had learned English from listening to the radio. As far as I was concerned, this guy was full of shit. I was even less eager to talk to him now. Cal, much to my building annoyance, continued his conversation with Tex, who told us we were likely to be sentenced to six years for illegal entry. He said there had been similar cases, and that's what they had received.

My heart sank.

By this time the barber had clipped off most of my beard, and I was about to get my first professional shave. He had a smooth touch and a steady hand. Amid all the gloom, it was nice to have such gentle treatment. After he had removed all the stubble, he took some white cream and smeared it on my face. It was a cool and soothing balm on my newly bald and sensitive face.

"Que es eso?" I asked wanting to know what the cream was. He replied that it was his secret ingredient.

I asked him again what it was, and his answer was undecipherable but drew laughs from the onlookers who had continued to arrive during our shaves and haircuts.

I asked Tex what the barber had said. "Hemorrhoid cream," he replied with a smile.

We returned to the holding cell and were given some hardboiled eggs. Then, after each of us had been asked a few elementary questions by one of the soldiers filling out forms, we were escorted outside of *La Cabaña* to another awaiting *aula*. This trip took 20 minutes and brought us to the base of a hill, which appeared to be in the center of Havana. The *aula* entered a guarded gate lined with an anchor fence and dropped us off at a building partway up the hill. This time we saw a portion of a large masonry structure on the summit. We were led past piles of reinforcing rods and welding equipment and entered a small office with a dark room. Photos were taken while we held a card printed with a number below our chins. Mine was *cuarento ocho, ciento vente siete:* 48127.

We were led outside and further up the steep hill. At the top we faced another drawbridge and moat. Above the main gateway was the inscription: *El Castillo del Príncipe* —the Prince's Castle.

Florida Today, Sunday, July 29, 1973

Persistence Finds Jax Man in Cuban Jail

JACKSONVILLE—A desperate mother and a persistent telephone operator have located a Florida man in a Cuban jail after two months of high-level diplomacy failed.

Mrs. Iris Longstreet of Jacksonville says she finally got word that her son was being held in a Havana prison by calling the jail and asking if he was there.

Chet Longstreet, 26, and three other Florida men were seized by Cuban authorities on May 26, Mrs. Longstreet said.

She said she had been getting only sketchy information from the U.S. State Department, which received information through the Swiss Embassy.

"I decided to try and call for myself and see if I could find out where he was being held," Mrs. Longstreet said.

She said she contacted an overseas operator in Miami Sunday and called the jail.

The Cuban operator at first insisted there was no jail in Havana, but the Miami operator said, "Listen, I know you have a jail there where they put people," Mrs. Longstreet said. "She was very nice. She wouldn't take no for an answer."

Mrs. Longstreet said she was finally put through to the jail where a spokesman confirmed that her son was being held. But she said she was not allowed to speak to her son.

"At least I knew he was alive. It was the best news I'd had," she said.

Mrs. Longstreet said she assumed the other three crew members were also imprisoned at the Havana jail.

The four were aboard a 65-foot shrimp boat on a cruise to Grand Cayman Island when they were seized by Cuban authorities.

Mrs. Longstreet said she was told by the State Department that the four were being held because Cuban officials claimed they found "suspicious items" including rifles, life rafts and a radio aboard the vessel.

Mrs. Longstreet said her son normally carried a pistol and the others had taken rifles in case they saw sharks while skindiving. She said the other items were usually aboard the boat. [The source of this indirect quote was never correctly identified.]

"My son and the others have never been involved in any Cuban-related activities," Mrs. Longstreet said. "There is no reason for them to be held."

Mrs. Longstreet said the Swiss embassy at first refused to help her contact her son when she made a personal plea.

"Finally, I said 'Can't you understand this is a heartbroken mother you're talking to?'" she said.

Then the official agreed to relay her message, she added.

"The message was that I love him and hope to see him soon," she said.

CASTILLO DEL PRÍNCIPE: AUGUST 10, 1973

We crossed the moat and entered the 200-year-old castle through a 2-story passageway at the base of a tower. At each end of this open-ended corridor was a row of 15-foot-high steel bars. Halfway up was a crosspiece below which were barred and locked gates. To the left of the entrance was a large administration room and on the right were two cell doors. We were escorted into the first door on the right—a holding cell for prisoners in transit, either coming in or going out. We waited there for an hour while the guards processed our files and returned the belongings we were not wearing. It was almost twilight. Some buckets of food were brought into the cell. We had a surplus of saffron-colored rice mixed with kidney beans and hard-boiled eggs. More prisoners had been expected, but they had not arrived. As we had had nothing except eggs the day before in G-2, we ate heartily.

A dozen more prisoners were now ushered in. Dan set to work trying to bum smokes, and he would share when he succeeded. Many of the prisoners were eager to share their limited supply of tobacco with the new American prisoners, and we began to sense that we had a degree of prestige among them. Occasionally a prisoner would pass the cell, peer in, point at us and say, *"Ah, Americana, un marijuanero, no?"* The implication went unnoticed until one of the prisoners in the tank informed us that there were at least one or two Americans inside the main part of the prison. The names Tony and Richard were mentioned repeatedly, as though they had fame and respect in the prison.

El Castillo del Príncipe—the Prince's Castle—is located on a hill overlooking the Plaza of the Revolution, the site of Fidel Castro's major public speeches. It was used as a prison until the mid-1970s. In 1982, it was named a UNESCO World Heritage site.

We were called out of the cell and conducted through a locked door directly behind the holding tank and proceeded up a staircase within the entrance tower to a door over which was inscribed *VIVAC*. This led to a long hall filled with three dozen prisoners. With our freshly cropped heads, white skins and spanking new prison uniforms, we stuck out like sore thumbs when contrasted with the dark-skinned Cubans in their faded uniforms. One of the older prisoners, a man of about 45, took an almost paternal interest in our welfare. He came over and spoke to us in limited English. He told us to listen for our names being called out after the other prisoners had returned from work and gave us a few smokes for which we were extremely grateful. He said we were going to be held in a section of the prison that was assigned to short-term prisoners and prisoners in transit. He further explained that many of the prisoners held in *VIVAC* worked on the immediate exterior grounds around the castle. They welded beds for the prison from the reinforcing rods we had seen earlier, baked bread for the people of Havana, and made furniture.

Soon, these working prisoners began to flood into the large room. Most of them were smoking long, thin hand-rolled cigarettes, which we called *spleeves*.

Once they had filed into the other sections, names of the new inductees at *Príncipe* were called. Soon we heard our names, though the pronunciation made it hard to recognize them. Mine sounded like *Gar—Dune Essa*. Chet's sounded like *Jet*. We answered the call and entered the large cell, which was filled with rows and rows of beds. A few of the Cubans, curious about the unusual opportunity to meet foreigners, clustered around us. Chet and I tried to deal with the questions in Spanish. Within an hour my head was swimming from the overload of concentration and recall necessary to understand the unfamiliar Cuban dialect.

The *s* sound was all but eliminated from most of the common words, and thus even the simple words and expressions I knew became unrecognizable. Probably one of the first phrases I had learned in high school was *Como estas?* This came out sounding like *Como eta?* which sounded more like Latin to me. Eventually, any conversation we had soon exhausted our vocabularies. Fortunately, there were a few Cubans who could speak limited English and we made small headway.

Many of the Cubans wished to discuss their favorite movies. It was obvious that many of them had developed a distorted concept of the U.S. from the films they had seen. One 15-year-old prisoner—whom we were told had attempted armed robbery at a bank—wanted to talk about the gangsters in the U.S. He kept looking at us with admiration—as though we were heroes and criminal veterans—and saying, "Whiskey. Women!" as if these were the tools of our trade and the only goals in life. Another inmate, who said he was jailed for six months for not working, wanted to talk about American movies he liked. I did okay translating titles of movies until he mentioned actor Lee Marvin in *Aquemaropa*. Literally, this means burnt cloth, but I could not think of any Marvin movie by that name. He went on for half an hour trying to get me to recognize what the film was. The following day I would learn that the title was Cuban idiom for *point blank*, meaning a gun's discharge so close that it could not miss its target. The burnt cloth reference was slang in Spanish of the cloth that was burned from the firing of a gun.

We slept on the hard floor that night without mattresses. My weight loss put my now-protruding bones in uncomfortable contact with the concrete floor. Just after dawn we heard the cry of *desayuno:* breakfast. It consisted of a roll and *leche con café*—sweetened condensed milk with a touch of coffee added for flavor. It was one of the few popular items on the limited menu at *Príncipe* We had no cups, but one was hospitably loaned to us, and the four of us alternated sips of the warm liquid.

Our names were called, and a guard led us to the second gate, which we had seen the previous day at the end of the main entrance. Our first view of the panorama of the prison was vivid and otherworldly. An immense open plaza—perhaps 250 feet across—was surrounded by five thick walls, each with large, barred doorways. Some served as gates to smaller courtyards flanked by subdivisions of cells; others were the windows to other cells. A quick scan of these dark openings suggested the prison consisted of about 10 large cells. Later I would learn there were about a dozen more. A large portion of the middle of the plaza was raised six inches above the perimeter of the concrete concourse. In the center of the terrazzo courtyard a giant star was inlaid; beneath the star was an inscription: *Prison de Habaña, 1936.*

Immediately in front of six of the cells were rows of chairs, half of them occupied by prisoners studying basic subjects such as reading, history and mathematics. Few of these students had any texts and lessons were apparently entirely taught by lecture.

As we crossed the great star in the courtyard in the blazing July sunlight, the prison was buzzing with the news of the new *Americanos.* As we passed the large, barred openings to the cells, arms, legs and faces of the occupants protruded. The prisoners reminded me of Goya's *Caprichios*—studies of the paupers, the aged, and the dissipated. The prisoners yelled the few words of English that were commonly known, "Hey, Joe, gimme won cigarette," and "Come here, Babee."

We were taken to the *botequin,* a first aid dispensary, by a trustee. I was glad to get into the shade where it felt 15 degrees cooler. Prisoner interns staffed the *botequin,* although one old prisoner doctor was present when we entered. Here a file noted our medical history, and we were given shots, presumably for tetanus. Then blood samples were taken.

For me, this did not go well. An intern was being taught how to draw blood. But he was having difficulty hitting the vein on the inside of my elbow. His hypodermic reminded me how much I hated getting shots as a kid. The needles then were almost as large in diameter as a pencil lead. These were apparently from the same vintage and were filed at a sharp angle so they would slice through the skin easily.

The intern's first attempt missed the vein entirely. He pushed it in again with no blood emerging and gave the needle a ghastly wiggle in an attempt to slice across the vein from the side. I made the mistake of watching him do this and became dizzy. His instructor came over at my yell and pulled the needle out. He reinserted the needle and obtained the sample correctly. As he withdrew the needle, a lump half the size of a golf ball began to form where the aborted attempt had taken place. I felt faint and was led to a bed where I rested for a few minutes until my head cleared.

When I finally got up, Chet was waiting at the entrance to the dispensary. We went outside to survey the courtyard as an intern approached to tell us that some Americans wanted to talk to us. He pointed 25 feet to our right, where three prisoners stood behind a large, barred gate leading to a 100-foot-long courtyard. They immediately evoked images of prisoners behind barbed wire at Auschwitz when the allies liberated the Jews—one had sores all over his face, another was rail thin with a yellow pallor. It was easy to guess that they were Americans. They gestured to us, and we went to meet them.

Stretching out their hands and smiling, the American inmates introduced themselves as Joe, Will and Jeff. Joe was the thin one. He had a large sharp nose with a small mouth and looked jaundiced. Will could easily have passed for James Cagney's kid brother, not only because of his appearance, but for his feisty demeanor. Only about 5 foot, 7 inches, he had dark features and an incorrigible personality. Jeff had a gruff rumble of a voice, distinctive blue-grey eyes, and a skin condition that looked like scurvy.

They told us they were *marijuaneros:* pot smugglers. They were there with a group of 12 other Americans, 10 had been taken in by the Cubans while smuggling marijuana, both by sea and air. They explained the other two prisoners were a hijacker named Lonnie and a crazed shrimp boat captain named Kevin. I realized I had joined a strange cast of characters in this isolated place unknown to most of the world.

We were told that we could expect to be lodged in the same cell with them shortly as we were summoned to the prison dining hall. Again, we passed the long wall of barred openings, meeting with new jeers and being called *marijuaneros* a few more times.

The dining hall consisted of a long hall bordered on one side by tall bars extending from elbow-level to the 14-foot ceiling. The tables were 30 feet long and constructed of smooth, formed concrete. We joined the end of a long line to get our food through a hole in the wall from which the trays were thrust. They were the same type we had used at G-2, only these were greasier. The day's food was *bacchanal,* an orange-colored pulpy fish that chewed like a combined mixture of bubble gum and hemp. It had a sour, putrid flavor and trying to swallow it was worse. We also got a portion of plain spaghetti, or *pagetti* as the Cubans called it. None of our group had eating utensils until a friendly Cuban noted our dilemma and produced two spoons, which we shared. All those grammar school lessons about germs and hygiene were suspended.

After the meal, we were led to Company 11, *Compania Once.*

This was where I met Roger, the third member of the crew on the boat with Will and Jeff. Of all the Americans I had met so far, he was the most striking. When I first spotted him, he was combing his black hair as if readying for a close-up photo. Instantly I thought of the World War II films with their stereotypical image of intrepid RAF pilots who had been shot down and were held in P.O.W. camps but remained chipper throughout. He appeared to be in excellent health and none the worse for his year in captivity. He had a sharp profile, luminous blue eyes, and wore what appeared to be a tailored prison uniform. His hair looked as though he was ready to do a Brylcreem commercial.

Roger and I immediately developed a rapport based on mutual interests. In the days and weeks to come, I would develop as strong a respect for him as I have ever had for another human being. He could be counted upon to do exactly the right thing in almost any situation.

I followed the group into what would become my prison home. My first view of the immense, L-shaped cell brought to mind images of the Black Hole of Calcutta and 18th-century debtors' prisons. Upon entering, the leg straight ahead was 175 feet and started out 70 feet wide and diminished to a point 5 feet wide. This was one of the points in the star fortification of the castle. There were three, large, barred openings through the 10-foot-deep exterior walls. Four people could sleep comfortably on the sill. The leg to the right was 70 feet wide and 250 feet long. To the left, on the outside intersection of the two legs of the cell, were five holes in the floor surrounded by waist-level walls—the toilets.

Another walled-in section—15 feet long by 4 feet wide—contained three spigots that protruded at head level. These showers were really just copper pipe poking out of the wall. A master external valve turned on the water three times a day, usually for less than 45 minutes.

Beds were made of welded concrete reinforcing rods draped with stretched canvas. Most of the beds were stacked three high. When we first entered the prison, 420 prisoners occupied the cell.

As I surveyed the immense cell in greater detail, I observed that the ceiling was 20 feet high and was illuminated by large bulbs. Numerous wires descended from the bulb wires and were connected to resistance coils set in gouged-out bricks. These were used as hot plates, primarily for preparing coffee and toasting rolls.

We now began to meet the other Americans. Chet, Cal, Dan and I split up and joined different groups of American prisoners, located in small clusters at diverse points within the cell. We were the source of news and information, so we were extended the best hospitality they could offer in a foreign prison.

The first group I met consisted of five people: Steve, Ralph, Richard, Jeff and Will. All were in their early 20s, with Richard being the youngest at 23; all had been sentenced to four years for smuggling marijuana.

The Cubans had captured Steve and Ralph when their sailboat, loaded with 100 pounds of marijuana, entered Cuban waters near a military installation off the south coast. They had become buddies while serving in the U.S. Army in Munich, and in the prison, rarely separated for more than 15 minutes. Ralph, who always looked as if he had just finished a month-long binge, was aptly nicknamed *Grog.* He could create humor out of almost any situation and took it upon himself to give everyone a nickname, including his partner, Steve, whom he called Orville for reasons unknown to the rest of us.

Richard, despite being the youngest, had the unenviable distinction of having been in prison longer than any of the other Americans in *Príncipe*—two years. His baby face, youthful exuberance and wire-rimmed glasses gave him the appearance of a boy genius. Grog had dubbed him *Skunk.* Richard had been discharged from the U.S. Navy and promptly became an ambitious and successful drug dealer, initially selling small quantities. But then he decided to go direct and smuggle in his own purchases.

The Cubans detained him and Vincent when they landed their rental plane, filled with marijuana, with notions of refueling in Cuba. Will and Jeff, along with Roger, had been in the process of transporting five tons of marijuana from Colombia when they lost both diesel engines on their 45-foot pleasure yacht. After drifting three days without power—and addled by sampling their wares—they had been seized in Cuban waters with their massive cargo. Jeff was called *Bruto,* apparently due to his superior handling of a Cuban in a fight at the shower line. Will, for reasons unknown, never acquired a nickname. They had just completed their first year in captivity; Grog and Orville would complete their first year within a week of our arrival.

During the first evening in *Once,* my attempt to update them on recent political, social and cultural events was interrupted by the cry of *recuento*—the nightly head count. Quickly the entire cell lined up beside their beds in rows of five. Those without beds, which included our crew, had to line up in front of the acrid air by the urinals in rows of ten. With eyes watering from the stinging odor, I watched three officers march through the cell at double time counting the rows and making notations on a clipboard. Then the cell returned to its earlier activity, though now it was at a more subdued level.

Roger and I talked until late in the night, mostly about music. We both had a strong affection for Joni Mitchell, who had released her *For the Roses* album just a few weeks before we left Florida. It taxed my brain to recall her poetic lyrics to *Cold Blue Steel and Sweet Fire,* a song about the derelict life of drug addiction. Finally, fatigue set in. It had been a long day. The American prisoners had chipped in to buy us mattresses since the prison officials did not provide them. I laid mine on the floor where I could find a space.

As I began to drift off to sleep, I had a peculiar sense of elation. At least now we could speak with people who would lay the facts on the line. Despite the discouraging nature of the American prisoners' statements about what we could expect, some had felt that the U.S. government would intercede on our behalf. Though not strong support, it was the first optimistic news we had heard since we returned to G-2.

DAY TO DAY: AUGUST 1973

In the morning, I was jolted awake by the yell of "*Recuento!*" The whole cell seemed panicky as I stumbled to the lines forming in front of the urinals. I tried to go back to sleep on my feet, I was so tired, but the bite of the urine fumes stung my eyes, and they began to water. Trustees marched through and checked that the columns of prisoners matched up with what they had on their clipboards. After a few minutes at attention, while they added the figures, it was all over, and they departed to give their attention to a new cell.

I returned to my mattress and rested without sleeping. Within 15 minutes Richard came over with a spare tin cup and hospitably invited me to join the group for *desayuno*, which was now being served. Feeling as though I had made the *Príncipe* social register, I walked over to the three bunk beds that defined their turf just in time to watch two prisoners drag what must have been a 20-gallon plastic container to their section of the cell. One of the two men at the handles of the container had a small tin cup on a stick, which he used to measure out portions of the *leche con café*. Everyone held out a cup for their daily allotment. Another man followed the bucket crew and handed out rolls. The veterans of *Príncipe* saved the rolls to be eaten later. I ate mine immediately.

Dan produced a sheet of fibrous paper, not unlike that used for newspapers, and proceeded to fold it and lick the crease so it would tear easily. I watched with fascination as he rolled it into a ball and then unfolded it. Once again he put another fold in the paper, which measured about five inches, and proceeded to pour the tobacco he had taken from a third of a Cuban cigarette along the crease. With experienced hands, he rolled a long joint-like *spleeve,* licked it secure, and lit it. After taking a few short, rewarding puffs, he passed it to his right. It made the circuit of seven people two times before it was just a pinch of discolored paper. Around the cell I saw many of the Cubans doing likewise—It was part of the ritual of life in *Príncipe.*

I spent several hours with this group and then moved to find out how the rest of the crew was doing. Dan and Chet had spent most of the previous evening and that morning getting acquainted with Joe, Henn, Roger and Lonnie.

Joe and Henn had been on a boat captained by Jay, a pleasure boater, who had feared the open water during a storm so much that he had run their boatload of marijuana into Cuban waters. It was obvious that Joe and Henn disliked Jay and held him responsible for the four years they must spend deprived of the warmth of their families. Henn was 45 years old, and Jay was a year or two older. They seemed like unlikely subjects to be involved in the drug-importing business, but I guess the promise of big profits tended to draw all kinds—the unfortunate, the bold and the clueless—into unlikely fields.

Henn was raised in Germany. He could recall listening to Hitler's radio broadcasts during World War II and came to the U.S. when he was 17 years old, after the post-war conditions became severe. His German accent added a weird ring to his Spanish and he gave Grog German lessons every day. It was Grog and Orville's intention to return to Germany immediately upon their release from confinement.

Henn was the craftsman of the Americans, and he could always contrive a way to make small and handy items—such as dice and cups—from such useless merchandise and trash as empty toothpaste tubes, plastic bags, tin cans and bottle caps.

Joe had been in the smuggling business for several years. At first, he was involved in smuggling pot by aircraft, but when the profit margin became substantial enough, he switched to boats. He explained that he had little to do with the actual setting up of these operations, but rather monitored them to make sure no one was "burned." He was a meek man who could credibly pass himself off as an accountant and somehow looked nothing like the soldier of fortune I expected to find in such risky business.

Lonnie had jet-black hair and dark eyes. According to his account, which had suspicious holes in it, he was a hijacker who came from the Chicago area. He was murky about his family background but gave the impression of having been the product of wealthy parents who were more preoccupied with their business and social lives than to devoting time to their only son. According to him, he had been shipped away to boarding schools most of his life and had been involved in radical political groups before being expelled from private schools. When not in school, he had been farmed out to his grandparents, and when he was old enough, he split and joined the Weathermen, a small but militant radical anti-war group. He was always vague about exactly what his role was, although he hinted it had something to do with a plan to dose the Chicago water supply with LSD. It turns out this was a slight distortion of the truth.

He struck me as a pathological liar, or someone who had a great deal to hide so people would like him. In reality, he had illusions of grandeur. Although I didn't know it at the time, it turned out he was the subject of the "R.I.S.E." chapter of *Toxic Terror: Assessing Terrorist Use of Chemical and Biological Weapons* by Jonathan B. Tucker. The book gives a vivid account of Allen Charles "Lonnie" Schwandner's real story, which included a youth spent in reform schools and a psychiatric hospital; an adolescence spent indoctrinated by a domestic terrorist group; and an attempt to help destroy mankind through the use of biological weapons—which ultimately brought him to Cuba, where he expected to be welcomed, but was imprisoned instead—all before he was 20 years old.

We spent the first morning in *Príncipe* meeting these Americans. Lunchtime was at 11 a.m. The other Americans all carried bags containing their valuables over to the corner where Richard's group was located and took turns guarding these items that would have brought a good price on the black market. One could never be sure of the purposes of individuals who remained behind at lunchtime, and previous experience had shown that items left unattended disappeared within this den of thieves.

The long line leading into the dining hall took us past eight other cells, which I had not seen before. While in the line, I took stock of the parapets 20 feet overhead. Guards with machine guns stood posted at each of the sections, which were divided by large barrier gates.

The guards on top covered the guards below who were on foot among the prisoners and were armed with dull and rusted machetes. The broad side of the blade made an effective weapon; the sharp side was even more effective in extreme cases as it could easily crack a bone.

Upon exiting *Once*, we followed a corridor around a block of small cells, each of which held probably 100 inmates. For meals, we would go to the right toward a gate that could seal off our cell and an adjoining one from the other zones. Upon passing through this gate, we turned left into another courtyard, which was subdivided by still another gated barrier. On either side of this gate were four cells. We also passed a barbershop flanked by guards who yanked people out of line who they felt were due for haircuts. Then a turn to the left led into the courtyard that ran along the wall of the dining hall. Each end of this courtyard was blockaded with heavy-duty gates controlled by guards. The prisoners waited between these gates after eating until either gate was opened.

On this, my first day in *Príncipe*, the guards, seemingly for mere amusement and to exercise their power, decided to open the gates and simultaneously charge the 400 prisoners from the other end with flailing machetes. Pandemonium resulted as the mob of prisoners pushed to get to the shelter on the other side of the 4-foot-wide opening.

In the scramble to avoid the sting of machetes, someone picked my pocket of a full pack of cigarettes, which the Americans had given me to purchase necessities. I made the sad discovery when I got back to the cell.

I noticed several prisoners eyeing my desert boots as we walked past them. Since shoes were nearly the only non-institutional clothing a prisoner had, they were a manifestation of wealth within the prison. My boots could be sold for a pack or two of cigarettes if I was lucky enough to locate an interested buyer. I began to look more closely at the other prisoners' footwear. Many had rather ordinary shoes that had been scored and then had leather thongs run through to give the shoe a different texture. Most wore poor-quality foam-bottom sneakers.

That afternoon I met with the men Cal had associated with earlier, Vincent and Jay. It seemed that these men, who had been most responsible for the mistakes leading to their group's capture, were drawn to each other. It didn't take me long to decide that the less time spent with them, the better.

Vincent was 32 years old and spoke with a high-pitched, effeminate voice. During the two years and several months he had been in captivity, he had completely let his body atrophy. He had nearly hairless, pale skin, spindly arms and—though he was not overweight—he had no muscle tone in his abdomen; his stomach bulged like a large bowl.

He had been the pilot of the small plane Richard had rented to transport marijuana. A fuel miscalculation led them to make a forced landing in the Cuban countryside and, oblivious to international relations, they thought they could fill a few gas cans, pay for the fuel, and take off again. They were apprehended and the 200 pounds of marijuana they had on board were discovered. Later it was learned that they had had enough fuel to reach Florida with little trouble.

Jay, with his heavyset body, thick five-o'clock shadow, and dark hair could easily have served as the inspiration for Fred Flintstone. Both he and Vincent seemed to spend most of the day on their bunks bartering for food or eating chocolate and cereal, drinking coffee or discussing sports. Their first question to Cal was who had won the Super Bowl seven months earlier.

I did little associating with Jay and Vincent as they appeared to be entirely negatively motivated and were resigned to whatever conditions the Cuban authorities would impose on them.

The remaining American in *Once* was Kevin, the 35-year-old shrimp boat skipper. He was easily the most solitary of the American inmates. In the years preceding his incarceration, he had made several trips to Cuba on various work and fishing vessels, and on a few of these trips, he had tried to speak personally with Fidel Castro to tell him how to run the country. Finally, one night he decided he couldn't wait to talk to Fidel about the things that were on his mind. Kevin said he "borrowed" someone's shrimp boat and singlehandedly navigated it to Havana where he was imprisoned. Kevin towered over the Cubans with his 6-foot, 3-inch lanky frame. He was an incurable nicotine addict and sold almost anything he had for a paltry two or three cigarettes and would spend hours scrounging around the massive cell looking for discarded cigarette butts, what the Cubans called *brevas*.

I began to wonder what I was doing with the likes of this group. Could I be the biggest loser?

CODES, CUSTOMS & CAUTIONS

Cigarettes were the prison currency. Prisoners could purchase four packs as often as every month and, when distribution was delayed, the value of the cigarettes increased substantially, offering a real study in simple economics and the laws of supply and demand.

The Americans received Red Cross packages through the Swiss officials three times a year. These contained valuable black market items, which could easily bring a good price in prison. The packages contained Fruit of the Loom briefs and T-shirts, Colgate toothpaste, toothbrushes, razors, Gillette blades, Halezone water purifying tablets, Tide detergent, and vitamins. The Americans would trade a few of their surplus items for as many as 15 or 20 cigarette packs. Inmates ranging in age from 15 to 70 were housed there and many of the older men would pay almost anything for the vitamins to supplement the deficient prison diet.

The diet was about 75 percent starch, in the form of rolls, rice, spaghetti and sugar. Fish composed about 15 percent of the menu and about 5 percent was meat. The rest of the diet was vegetables and jelly. We would receive citrus about once or twice a month. At times, the skin on the fruit was so black and the inside so pale that it could not be determined if we were eating a lime, an orange or a dwarf grapefruit.

Most of the Cubans could visit with their families once every two to four weeks and they would eat picnic lunches, which their families prepared with great care. At one time, the Americans could join friends for these family visits. But this practice had stopped several months before our arrival—perhaps because it either encouraged black market exchanges or interfered with them. Because there was so much secrecy, many conversations were mere speculation of why something *had* happened, what *was* happening, or what *would be* happening.

Once a month, the inmates could receive *java* bags from their families and friends. These were burlap bags loaded with cake, chocolate, cookies, grains, sweetened condensed milk, coffee and bread. The Americans often bought these food items with the cigarette packs they had acquired trading the items supplied by the Red Cross. They would also do their shopping for foodstuffs, blankets, clothing, cups, spoons and mattresses when cigarettes were in strong demand. The Americans were excellent capitalists, working market fluctuations to their advantage.

This became even more evident—and metaphorical—when they played the epitome of imperialistic games, RISK, where they would try to control continents.

Life in the cell was predictable. In the mornings, and again late in the afternoons, all movement throughout the cell came to an abrupt halt as the floor was mopped. This consisted of a team of 10 men splashing water on the floor and sliding the dirt and spit around with filthy rags draped over a crosspiece nailed to a pole, thus creating a mop. The prisoners who did the mopping took this cosmetic job seriously. Anyone moving in the aisles during this operation was cursed at by Netti, the cell trustee. He was also the man to pay off for a bed, a mattress or extra milk in the morning. He was about 5 feet, 5 inches tall, had only canine teeth, and was notorious for being a *bugaro*—a bugger.

Showers in *Once* involved a lesson in procedure. Among all the *Americanos,* there were only three pairs of shower sandals, which were shared informally. Wrapping a towel around one's waist and carrying a bar of soap, one proceeded to the line forming at the running spigots. The prospective showerer would then yell out, "*Quien es el ultimo?*"—who is the last one in line? The person who had preceded you replied "*Aqui*" or "*Yo.*" As the line moved along, slowly arguments would occasionally flare up over who had swiped whose soap when their eyes were soaped up. After about three minutes under the cold water, one would begin to get dirty looks from those waiting in line.

After my first shower in *Príncipe,* I discovered that toweling off had its own form of decorum. In American locker rooms, one faced their locker as they dried off—not so in *Once.* As I faced the wall, exposing my buttocks, Grog said offhandedly, "You shouldn't do it like that." He then gestured to look behind me—five faces filled with questionable motives were contemplating what they considered to be an invitation. I turned around really fast!

The vermin of *Príncipe* added to the daily hassles and discomfort of cell life.

Cockroaches were in such abundance that no one bothered to try to eliminate them. At night, the two-story walls of *Once* looked like large specks moving randomly. They were creepy at best.

Chinchas were far more of a nuisance. These tiny bloodsuckers hid in the shadowy creases of the canvas tied to beds and in the joints of the concrete reinforcing rods welded together to form the bed frame. Once they found a host, they would crawl along, stopping to bite several times along the journey. Their path left a series of red marks, and for some with strong reactions, large lumps. They itched unrelentingly. And they caused unusual phenomena. Each new bite made the other recent bites itch all over again. In an attempt to minimize the bugs, many people put the legs of their beds in tin cans filled with water. This seemed to prevent them from crawling up from the floor; however, if a friend who was a "carrier" sat down on your "sanitary" bed, the pests could cross over the "island" and infest the bed. Every Saturday was bed-burning day: the canvas was unstrung, and flammable items were ignited and directed at the *chinchas'* hiding places. Some beds seethed with hundreds of the just-hatched, near-microscopic white bugs. I got chills up my spine every time I saw how fast they could reproduce. And they turned red when they ate.

The worst of the vermin infesting *Príncipe* were the *caraganos*—a type of body lice that were nearly impossible to eliminate; anyone infested with them was referred to as a *caraganero*. Fortunately, I did not have any direct contact with these creatures, perhaps because I was forewarned of the suspected *caraganeros* by Richard.

Rats were plentiful in the prison and often would scurry boldly around the prison at night as if they owned the place, using sewage tunnels beneath the toilet holes as their main paths. It was unnerving to be positioned over the hole and hear them running about chattering.

Time was spent, day-to-day, playing chess, reading, sewing and studying Spanish. At night, we played bridge, told stories, made coffee and cooked rolls. For reading material, the Americans had about a dozen books in English. Some were pulp Westerns and mysteries such as *Gun Quick, Restless Border, Have His Carcass* and *The Lenient Beast. The Sea Raider Atlantis* was a book about the World War II German vessels designed for quick makeovers so they could approach Allied ships under false national flags and then sink them when the pretense succeeded. The finer literature included *Tale of Two Cities, Anatomy of a Murder, Moby Dick* and last, and rather appropriately, *Lost Horizons*. The paperbacks had almost all been read several times by each of the Americans and were dog-eared. When the binding gave out, the book would be placed in an envelope, which often resulted in the pages being out of sequence, prolonging the whole reading process. Sometimes critical pages were missing—aggravating.

Richard's group was composed of avid card players. Bridge was the standard nightly game although occasionally it would be poker or RISK. When they found out about my art background, I was promptly recruited to draw designs for the cards and playing boards. Henn outdid himself by casting dice for other board games like Parcheesi by melting down plastic bags into a mold constructed from an old zinc toothpaste tube. Once the bar of brown plastic had cooled, he cut it into square blocks, rounded the corners, and gouged small indentations he filled with toothpaste so they would show up white. They worked surprisingly well. As games of chance were outlawed in Cuba, penalties were administered to anyone playing anything other than chess or checkers. The Americans' attitude was, "What are they going to do, throw us in prison?"

During our first few weeks in *Once*, I rarely left the cell except for meals. Will was taking classes, so he had an opportunity to scope out events taking place in other parts of the prison. His studies consisted of studying Spanish with the Cubans, and he was proud of the fact that he had gotten all the way to fourth grade before they prohibited Americans from taking these classes.

One day I was allowed to accompany Richard to the *botequin;* I had been constipated for a week. Jeff who had reportedly not gone to the toilet for 30 days set the record for constipation. Such changes in regularity were not uncommon because of the heavy rice and spaghetti diets. We got a bottle of laxatives and then went over to what was known as the Translation Department. There, Cubans with a good command of English translated various professional journals published in English—mostly psychology-related. One I noticed was about the benefits of withholding foods in interrogation settings. I assumed these translated articles were turned over to G-2 so that they could replicate the successful techniques to make their procedures more effective.

While at the Translation Department, Richard arranged the sale of my desert boots for two packs of cigarettes. As part of the exchange, I received a pair of Cuban sneakers, which were terribly uncomfortable. Since I had few opportunities to walk more than a hundred feet 23 hours a day, it did not seem like a great sacrifice. When we left there we returned to *Once,* and I celebrated the purchase by buying the basic items I needed—a cup, spoon, sheet and towel.

Not long after arriving in *Príncipe,* I learned about other Americans being held in other sections. One was Anthony, an articulate Black in his early 30s from the San Francisco Bay area. He had felt that the oppression of Blacks and other minorities would disappear in a society such as Cuba, which reportedly was based on economic equality, so he hijacked a commercial airliner and robbed the passengers. This was his big mistake. Robbery was a crime and disqualified him from receiving political refugee status, and he was sentenced to 10 years. Anthony was the best American chess player in *Príncipe,* but he chose to associate with the Cubans and our contact with him was infrequent, but cordial.

Upon the parapets of the castle were a hospital, medical laboratories and, in the center of the prison—far away from any exterior walls—a small, high-security cell. Frank, the longest imprisoned of the veteran American prisoners, was held in the hospital. I was told he was wanted in Florida for armed bank robbery. After taking a half-hour course in flying, he rented a plane, packed his wife and infant, and fled to Havana. As soon as he landed, he and his small family were separated, and he was placed in solitary confinement in G-2 for one and a half years. During that time, he was subjected to several bizarre psychological tortures: For days on end, a squeaky fan was placed close to his cell; he was given injections of sodium pentothal and other drugs with strange side effects; he was kept awake for long stretches. His health declined. He never found out what had happened to his wife and child.

Later I would learn that the Cubans suspected he worked for the CIA when he came to the island in 1963.

I never got to meet Frank, but the incredible circumstances of his experiences at the hands of the Cubans left me in awe of the man. As he and Henn were approximately the same age and had spent time together in the hospital, they frequently sent messages to each other, using orderlies and interns as their couriers, developing a strong friendship over their years of captivity.

Before the number of American prisoners grew too large, they had been confined to the parapets of the castle. This was, for all practical purposes, the penthouse section of the prison and now it was populated largely by doctors, most of whom had been caught trying to flee to the U.S. Most of them spoke English fluently and they always had enough cigarettes. Their food was also slightly better.

The parapets offered a grand view of Havana and sunlight was abundant. However, after Henn had gotten high on a variety of medications he pilfered from the meager pharmacy, the Americans were moved into the general population of the prison. Frank stayed behind because of the physical effects of his time in solitary confinement.

In August, I learned that the Americans had managed to get letters to their relatives and friends via the Cuban postal service, although delivery was never certain, and it was always delayed anywhere from three weeks to six months. It was extremely hard, but I finally began to write a letter to my parents on Sunday, August 26, 1973. Not knowing their circumstances or health troubled me greatly. I only knew that I needed to reassure them that I was all right and be optimistic about our hoped-for release in "a few months." Any detailed information regarding our circumstances jeopardized the letter getting past the censors, so the rest of my letter was vague and contained little information. I numbered my letters with Roman numerals, starting with 1. This way, I hoped my parents would be able to keep track of what was not getting through to them. This first letter began like this:

Sunday, August 26, 1973

Castillo de la
Príncipe Vedado, Zapata
Zona 3, Compania 11
La Habana, Cuba

Dear Mom & Dad,

This will be a short letter to let you know that I am in good health and as well as can be expected in the present situation.

I assume that Mona has given you a rundown of our situation and kept you informed of the slight information we've managed to transmit to her. We have been kept in the dark about our future here, so there is little I can tell you at this point. All we know is that we have not been charged with anything, and we have been told of no court date. Experience has taught us that things move deceptively slowly here.

We've been told that letters may take anywhere from five weeks to three months to be transmitted, so communication will be of a limited and awkward nature. Since the mail service seems unreliable and delayed, I'll keep this letter short. My letters shall be numbered, and I'll try and keep a copy of each.

Please let me know when this letter arrives; shortly I hope to be permitted a telegram.

My being held here would not be so bad if I had some reassurance that you are both okay. I pray that you are in good health and ask that you forgive me for the worry I must be causing you. My greatest concern until I return is for the two of you. Unfortunately, I seem to realize my errors when I'm in a position least likely to correct them.

Please take care of yourselves and give my love to Gayle, Carol-Lou and the kids. Until I return,

All my love,
Gordon

This first letter reached my parents exactly three months later, just days after Thanksgiving.

Prison culture in Cuba had its unique codes and cultures. For the most part, altercations within the gigantic cell were inevitable with as many as 400 prisoners confined at any given time. Fights were hardly violent, except when someone mentioned their opponent's mother in unflattering terms, the highest form of insult to the Cubans. Usually, though, fighting followed a predictable ritual; first, some yelling would be heard coming from a distant part of the cell, the speech would accelerate and increase in volume, and then finally it would be interrupted by the sound of hands slapping flesh.

These slaps would go on for several seconds as the other prisoners climbed up on their beds for a ringside seat. In a few moments, it was all over and both parties went away feeling some degree of satisfaction.

Within the prison, and on the street, an active and outlawed religion called *Abaqua* was practiced, which had its roots in African myths and legends with voodoo-like superstitions. The religion was more like a fraternal gang. Often at various spots in the prison, graphics that resembled serpentine arrows with different types of cross markings could be seen. Many of the Black inmates had these markings tattooed on their arms and backs. *Abaqua* devotees were responsible for at least four murders in the prison in one week. It was part of their code that if a friend or a blood brother was injured or killed, his assailant must be dealt with. The assailant, knowing this, would then seek out the one who was seeking him out. It turned into a deadly cat-and-mouse pursuit.

As I returned to the courtyard outside our cell one day after eating the noon meal, *almuerzo*, and was trying to grab a few rays of sunlight before being sent back into the gloom of the cell, I heard a shout. I turned and saw a short, Black Cuban charge a young, thin Black.

The Cuban held a triangular piece of folded tin can in his fist and was using it like a dagger. The tall youth could only walk backward in terror as the short one punched him repeatedly in the abdomen with the crude, but effectively sharp, instrument. In a few seconds, his assailant fled through the open gate, looking over his shoulder as he ran. The stricken victim looked at the holes in his shirt. As he put his hands over the wounds in his abdomen, blood ran between his fingers. I saw him go into shock, then his legs began to buckle, and he folded down. His face looked as if his body was betraying him. His friend rushed up and half walked and half carried him to the *botequin* as blood splattered behind them. During the following week, we saw more blood in the other courtyards, evidence of a continuing vendetta.

From this experience, I learned it could be lifesaving to always have some kind of implement or cloth as a buffer against any attacks. I got into the habit, after removing my shirt, of tucking it into the waist of my blue denim pants. It would later prove to be a good idea.

GRIEVANCES: SEPTEMBER 1973

The veil of sleep lifted momentarily. From his bunk, which seemed far away in my semi-conscious state, I heard Roger say, "They've all got it." Seconds later I felt a stirring in my bowels. I drifted back to sleep again. I had been up very late the previous night and did not move again until lunchtime. Halfway to the dining hall, I felt a sharp pain in my entrails. By the time I began to eat, cramps had set in, and I no longer wanted food. As I started the walk back to the cell, searing pain hit full force and I doubled over. It was so sudden and potent that I could not walk for a few seconds. By the time I reached the cell, I felt like my core would explode through my posterior. What made matters worse was there was a line of 10 people waiting at each of the five toilet stalls.

Gripping my knees until my hands were bone white, I fought off the impulse to throw pride and hygiene to the wind and satisfy the fundamental desire to explode like a volcano. Others felt the force punch into their abdomen and bowels so strongly that they could hold out no longer. With all sense of dignity forsaken for relief, they squatted over the wash basin and a large crack in the center of the cell and let it all come. The desire to join them was overwhelming, but I held off the pain for long minutes with eyes clenched and experienced something close to ecstasy when I finally got into one of the private stalls. Never had I felt such a mixture of pain and pleasure simultaneously. As it turned out, the previous night's squash had been contaminated. More than 400 inmates were afflicted with dysentery, which wasn't uncommon, although this time it was on a large scale.

Three days later, the prison rumor wire spread the news that more Americans were coming. They turned out to be more smugglers.

We met them later that day. Their boat *Breeze Dream* had run into Cuban waters containing a box of cocaine worth thousands of dollars and a chunk of hash the size of a softball. It was crewed by Robert, a 40-year-old skipper, two other men in their early 20s, and a 25-year-old woman—an unlikely collection. Robert was from San Francisco and was an adventurer, traveling about the Caribbean and South America on his sailing sloop. His crewmen were David and Davis.

David had become involved in the whole smuggling scheme to prove his dedication to a girlfriend who was backing the operation with another boyfriend's money. Previously, he was involved on the fringe of radical political groups from the Washington, D.C., and Philadelphia areas. Because he was the youngest American prisoner and was incredibly awkward, he was called *The Kid.*

Davis was a former lieutenant in the Army, and he didn't have any of the stereotypical drug runner or drug-user characteristics. How he got involved in the whole smuggling venture was never clear to me. He considered himself an authority on almost every subject and quickly added to the frictions that developed daily. He was from the Midwest and could easily have hired out as an underpaid freelance bore.

We soon learned that the woman who had crewed with them was at a woman's prison called *Nueva Manajay,* New Dawn. Robert's imprisonment was even more difficult for him to accept as he was in love with her. Later I learned that the conditions at *Nueva Manajay* were supposed to be even worse than the ones we were enduring.

The crew of the *Breeze Dream* quickly became oriented to the conditions that had confounded us a mere six weeks earlier. When our group first arrived at the prison, it had taken us three weeks to obtain vacant beds. As there was a big change in the population of *Once* shortly thereafter—most likely due to a work project—the newcomers got out of sleeping on the floor within a week. Their timing was fortuitous because, right after they got their beds, there was a big influx of prisoners. Within two weeks, the population went from 275 to 420. Chet figured that out to an average of 18 square feet per inmate. With the increase in population came quick tempers and high tensions.

In between all these distractions, I located an envelope and the postage to mail a second letter to my parents. I tried to make them believe that we were not going to be in Cuba much longer, figuring this would keep them hopeful—and because my intuition told me it would not be that long.

Two weeks later, I sent my first letter to Lorna. The tables had turned, in a sense, and now I was the needy one.

Sunday, October 7, 1973

Dear Lorna,

To try and send you my thoughts & feelings at this uncertain time and place is nearly futile from the outset, but I at least want you to know that I'm okay and that I miss you.

My initial concern is to get a letter to you, so I will be short on details of the last 4½ months. I hope to convey more from a later, closer, vantage point.

At present, all I know for certain is that we're here for an indefinite period that may amount to a few weeks or many months. Beyond that, we know almost nothing. We can only hope that this whole mess will be straightened out soon, and we'll be returned quickly.

Since we left the day after I last wrote, I've spent much of my time thinking about you. I wonder, among many misty thoughts, if you are still in Hawaii or have returned to the mainland. It's a difficult time-distance to be held off at, but it provides me with many previously unaccepted realizations. You'll probably wonder what the last statement means & more elaboration by me would be unwise. Sorry!

For now, I'm filling the time in by designing lava-cut domes for the slopes of Hawaii, reading the few English books available, learning to swear in Spanish, and trying to recall the lyrics and melodies of Joni Mitchell, Elton John, Jethro Tull, Leonard Cohen, Dylan, Emerson Lake & Palmer and the Stones. Remembering the lyrics to songs I know so well has been excruciatingly frustrating for the most part. If you're up to a favor or two, and I'm here long enough, I'd appreciate a transcript or two.

I understand that mail service is intermittent & delayed—anywhere from three weeks to three months—so I'll wish you the very best belated wishes for your birthday.

There is much I want to say, Lorna, but it will be best said in the future. I hope you've kept in contact with Mona and that she's lifted a few of the questioning clouds about everything. I also hope you're with good and caring company. I look forward to the possibility of an early, happy reunion.

I'll try to write again soon.

Always love,
Gordon

During this time the entire cell was called out for inoculations. As each prisoner's number was called, he stepped forward and was administered a vaccination. The needles were not sterilized after each shot. When it came time for the members of the *Silver Sands* to be vaccinated, Richard explained to the officials that we had received our shots just two months earlier. None of us wanted to take a chance on those needles. Fortunately, for once, the officials were reasonable and let us pass back into the cell without getting the shots.

Due to a number of similar problems that had become more apparent as time passed, the American prisoners began to compile a list of grievances—inequities in the system—for the prison administrators. We were not allowed to visit with our families. We could not receive packages from anyone. We could not participate in work details and earn benefits. We were limited in our capacity to deal with the Cuban prisoners due to the language barrier. We received mail on an extremely intermittent basis. And other inmates had stolen a sizeable number of our personal items.

I was largely responsible for composing this letter; translation was argued over by Lonnie and Richard who were undoubtedly the most fluent in Spanish. After it was signed by the Americans, it was hand-delivered to one of the prison section chiefs during the first week of October. We received not one word of response, so we began work on a second, but brief, letter to the officials requesting a meeting with them.

RIOT: OCTOBER 1973

With the increase in the inmate population—more than 400 in our cell alone—problems regarding territory became more pronounced. By now, Henn, Joe, Dan, Chet, Roger and I had two adjacent triple-decker bunks. The six of us would sit on the bottom beds, facing each other and talk, drink coffee, and smoke cigarettes. When we returned to the cell after every lunch, the aisle space between the beds had decreased. Lonnie ended up speaking to the Cubans in the next row, and they agreed to stop moving our beds closer together. A mark on the floor was drawn to determine the beds' locations, but they continued to move our beds together until there was almost no room left to move between them.

Before this problem was resolved, all the prisoners were called out of their cells, section by section. We were taken to the star courtyard and told to strip. While we were doing this, teams of guards went through *Once*, emptying the bags containing our personal belongings, smashing glass items, and confiscating any improvised knives or blades. They also removed a large number of reinforcing bars that appeared during more serious arguments. Packs of cigarettes were also pilfered.

The whole cell was then sprayed with a chalky liquid, which was supposed to be insecticide. We decided the spraying was only effective when the bugs drowned in it. Then, carrying our clothing in our arms, we were made to run up to a line of guards who searched our clothing for more contraband. We were then permitted back into our cell to clean up the damage left behind by the ransackers. This whole process was referred to as *cordillera*.

Everyone was disturbed by the search havoc, which was more destructive than anything else. Numerous contraband items were left undiscovered or ignored.

Everything, including our beds and clothing, was soaked with the insecticide. Grumbling was prevalent and everyone's mood turned foul.

The cell had returned to some kind of semblance of order by lunchtime. Beds had been washed free of the insecticide, and the spilled contents of our bags had been repacked and hung off the beds.

When we returned from lunch, we noted that our beds had once again been pushed together, so Chet and I began to push the three-tier beds back to the agreed-upon spot. All of a sudden, the beds lurched angrily back toward us and a torrent of Spanish swearing and gibberish accompanied it. I walked from the aisle between the bed to the wider aisle at the foot of the beds and tried to communicate to the lanky Cuban that the bed had been moved beyond the mark on the floor. Our command of Spanish dwindled as we tried to reason with the inmate. He continued his unintelligible stream and constantly referred to himself as being defiant and *guapo*.

Guapo, in *Príncipe*, meant tough. It was one of the hierarchies of self-assertive phrases often used by the Cuban inmates in challenges. When they began, the cell instantly quieted so the declaration now became a point of public pride and honor. There was even an escalation ritual for would-be combatants. Often a prisoner would state "*Soy pingu!*" Loosely translated, this meant "I have a big dick." It was meant to convey that the speaker was a mean and powerful person not to be trifled with. The rejoinder, or superlative form of this expression by one not willing to back away, was *Soy moringu*. This asserted the speaker had a "very big dick" and escalated the encounter, usually announced by the sounds of vicious slapping and blows to each other's bodies. It was almost like a sissy prison with juvenile name-calling.

The black Cuban Chet and I faced began to state he was *pingu*. As he continued vehemently, I moved the beds to the mark on the floor. Obviously, our words were having little effect upon his display of how *pingu* he was; he was spoiling for a fight. He disappeared for a moment behind the row of beds. The dim light of the cell and backlighting made it difficult to see him clearly when he emerged and violently slammed the beds back, ending our access to them. I kicked the beds back.

"Take that, you sonuvabitch," I yelled with no thought. That did it.

In the dim light, I saw his arm move forward, and a small glass bottle whistled by my ear harmlessly. I pulled my shirt from where it hung in my waistband and began to wave it in his face, suspecting he had more to throw. He did have another bottle and was getting ready to throw it. I obstructed his view and fouled his aim as the second missile fell wide of its mark. I thought he had expended his arsenal and went in for a body tackle into the beds. But I was wrong. As I charged, the Cuban swung full force with a heavy Mason jar he had hidden behind his back. It hit me just behind my left eye and above the ear. I felt my skull dent and saw a blast of bright light at the moment the jar shattered. Momentarily stunned, I put my hand to the wound and felt blood and sharp glass shards intermingled in my scalp. My anger rushed to fury, and I tore off after the assailant as he ran away. I got no more than 10 feet when I was collared from behind as the Cuban's ally dropped down from a bunk, nearly pulling me to the floor. By the time I wrestled free, the aisle was jammed with prisoners and further pursuit was futile. I began to crumble.

Within minutes, Netti, the cell trustee, had me at the gate to the cell and was calling for a guard. I was taken to the *botequin* where most of the glass particles were removed from my scalp and the cuts were doused with red antiseptic. While still groggy, I was then taken to the Section Administration Office. My assailant was there with the prison section chief. We were both castigated for being involved in the incident and summarily deprived of two visits with our families. Obviously, that was going to hurt him a lot more than me. It could have been worse, the chief said; we could be placed in the infamous *Zona Uno*. This was commonly referred to as *Los Leoneros*, or the "Lion's Den," reserved for the worst and most cutthroat prisoners.

Treatment and conditions there were rumored to be medieval.

By the time we returned to *Once*, all I wanted to do was lie down. My head felt like it had been walloped by a pile driver as the three-inch wide lump on the side of my head blossomed.

I rested for a while, but the conversation of the Americans in the adjacent beds began to disturb me. They were saying that this fight was significant because, in all earlier confrontations, the Americans had come through as the definite victors. In mine, I had not had the upper hand when it was over. Up to this point, the Cubans held the Americans in awe and with a degree of fear. We were rumored to be karate experts, an unearned reputation, but to our advantage. Now, the Americans were saying, the other inmates were becoming more challenging and cockier. They began to pressure me into a rematch, taking on my Cuban assailant and re-establishing the supremacy the Americans had enjoyed.

My head continued to feel like it was splitting open.

By nightfall, it had been planned for me that I was to take on the Cuban as soon as possible. The Americans, or at least half of them, were to keep the other inmates from interfering in the fight. I told the other Americans that I would do it, but it had to be when and where I wanted. They had to point him out to me since I had never gotten a good look at him in the poor light. He was about 20 years old, an inch shorter than me and thin. He was hardly a formidable opponent—but I was down to about 150 pounds—hardly an imposing adversary.

About an hour went by with everyone waiting for me to go after this guy. I insisted on waiting until he came down the aisle without any of his companions. Chet and Lonnie insisted I was stalling. Like Shakespeare's Iago in *Othello,* Lonnie, who was happiest when instigating turmoil and trouble, went off to another section of the cell and told some Cubans that we were going to "tear ass." Word spread rapidly. Soon many of the inmates, particularly the Blacks, began to strut by and say they were *guapo* and could kick our asses. The cell filled with electricity. It seemed that the full moon was breeding lunacy.

By now the Americans thought nothing was going to happen, and they went to other parts of the cell. It was then that my target appeared in the aisle exactly where I wanted him. No one was ready but me.

I flew out from the alley of our beds and ran up to the Cuban at full tilt. He didn't see me until an instant before I smashed him in the face, and he reeled as I threw more blows.

He ducked, defensively grabbing me about the waist and back. His head was under my arm, avoiding the full force of my punches; the only way I could effectively break his hold was by backing him into one of the massive support columns.

I looked up momentarily from this peculiar waltz of revenge and was transfixed as the cell exploded with action, as though a flame had come into contact with gasoline vapor, unleashing pent-up fury. In front of the showers, Chet was punching a Cuban as Grog swung two into the toilet stalls. Richard and Will were upending another into the 55-gallon drum used as a garbage can. My opponent continued to scurry around as I tried to break his grip around my waist by backing into beds, columns and walls. Lonnie came bounding off a bunk bed onto the back of a Cuban. The air was filled with sneakers, tin cups and mop poles thrown by the approving but more cautious audiences. They treated this as a sporting event where they had ringside seats. It was hard to tell who was on whose side. Lonnie, like a buccaneer in a pirate movie, bounced off a bed like it was a trampoline, and then rolled a 55-gallon drum down an aisle to slow down onrushing Cubans. As I swung by my adversary, Bill and Grog were stuffing Cubans into the urinals. It was a real riot.

Moments later, whistles sounded and the cell almost froze. Then the prison inspector entered with a phalanx of six guards with machetes who walked through a mess of tin cans, torn paper, towels, overturned barrels and beds, and small plastic items. He went directly over to Lonnie and asked what happened. Then he accused Lonnie of instigating the entire incident. He told him things were going to be very hard for him. Then he summoned all the active American participants to the section office. His manner was punitive and unyielding.

The inspector in the section office lined us up and told us that we would not be permitted to carry on in this manner. When he was told of our letter of grievances—of which he was either uninformed or had neglected to read—he began to reply in enigmatic statements, proudly quoting titles of English literature and phrases from Shakespeare, attempting to convince us that he was erudite. As Henn tried to describe the problems that were unique to the American prisoners, the inspector interrupted with criticism of our actions. Joe, who was normally soft-spoken, insisted that the cell was now extremely hostile and further problems were inevitable. He said he would not spend another night there.

We were discharged from the section office with the inspector's puzzling closing reply, "It will be as you like it."

Back in the cell, we all went over what had taken place during the riot and the outcome; we were viewed with new respect by the Cubans. Many of the older prisoners who had been on our side throughout the fracas said they had not enjoyed anything so much in all their years of captivity. Ten Americans had fought off more than 25 Cubans and re-established their previous reputation of worthy scrappers unwilling to walk away from a fight. It was a small reward.

My head hurt for the next month.

Back in the States, news from a New Jersey Congressman was almost as bleak.

October 15, 1973

Congress of the United States House
of Representatives Washington, D.C.

Honorable Benjamin H. Mabie
769 U.S. Highway No. 9
Bayville, New Jersey

Dear Ben:

Thanks very much for your recent letter relative to Gordon Hess. *(sic)*

This is truly a heartbreaking case, and quite frankly, I have no encouraging news at this time.

Less than two weeks ago, several Cuban refugee boats, well-armed, entered Cuban territorial waters, and attacked two Cuban fishing boats. Since that time, the Swiss officials have been provided any and all information.

I further understand that the Swiss have not been given permission to visit any of the American prisoners or deliver any mail, and that which had been given to the Cubans for delivery was returned.

Consequently, about the only hope the Hess family has is to write directly to the Cuban Government, the Ministry of Foreign Affairs in Havana. But I hold out no hope that it will be delivered, personally.

I truly regret that circumstances are such that I cannot forward any encouraging news; however, rest assured, when I have any information at all, I will see to it that Mr. And Mrs. Hess are notified immediately.

Thanks again for writing, and with all best personal regards.

Sincerely,
Charles W. Sandman, Jr.
Member of Congress

ZONA UNO: OCTOBER 23, 1973

The day following the riot, the Americans gathered and discussed what needed to be done since there was no response from the officials about our concerns; they were turning a deaf ear to the Americans' problems. Despite protests by some of the group, it was decided that our situation had to be emphasized further. We drew up a short letter stating conditions in *Once* had become intolerable and jeopardized our safety; we would not return to the cell after dinner and would sleep outside the cell if necessary. The letter was delivered at lunchtime.

Everyone supporting this action began to roll up their bags, clothing and blankets. The Cuban inmates watched us with interest. The inmates had never submitted such demands to the officials in the past. Sensing that our actions might encourage the rest of the prison to be more demonstrative, we were quickly summoned to the section office again. We were told they had located a cell that would accommodate some of our wishes and would isolate us from the prison populace. We were moving that evening.

With a clatter, we pushed our beds, now heaped with bags, tin cans, chess boards, books, rope and other paraphernalia over the curbing in the courtyard outside of *Once,* and began our exodus through the corridors of two-storied walls. As we speculated where we were going, a few of the beds fell awkwardly apart from the weight as we crossed curbs along the star courtyard, the prison's largest open space. We followed the section official several hundred feet to our new and previously unknown destination, *Zona Uno,* the castigation zone.

Passing through a 10-foot-tall gate, we entered a courtyard about the size of a bus.

There were two cell doors on each side. Three of them led to cells containing the *maricónes,* the homosexuals. The fourth door led to our new quarters. Directly opposite the gate entering the zone was the cell door that led to the Lion's Den, the punishment cells. This was immediately next to and at a right angle to our new cell. It would be more accurate to describe it as a dungeon.

Entering our cell, centuries of mildew greeted us—hitting us squarely in the face with a cool misty and humid odor. The cell had two openings: the door with a barred window and a ventilation shaft in the barrel-vault ceiling. The chamber was 30 feet long and less than 20 feet wide. It had two spigots and two toilets, similar to those in *Once,* along the side of the cell entrance. Within days, our few leather items grew mold and became nearly useless.

The *maricónes* smiled at us as we moved in. They were the happiest people we had yet seen in Cuba and enjoyed flirting with us. With a great deal of clanging, we moved our metal-framed beds into the cell. Five Cubans—who had either worked for G-2, the police or prison officials as *chibas,* i.e. stool pigeons, and whose survival and safety among the prison populace was doubtful—already lived there. The trustee of the cell, a former G-2 official who had used his position to rob a home, was immediately labeled *Jefe,* or Chief. He spoke English well and was an imposing presence in physique and demeanor, standing just over 6 feet. I guessed he must have been in his 40s. He

We spent two months in a dark, gloomy and moldy dungeon similar to this one. (Photo taken in a St. Augustine, Florida, fortress.)

asserted himself quickly and later said his 20-year-old sidekick was his nephew, a 5-foot, 3-inch curiosity named Israel, and as the days passed, we became suspicious of their relationship. The other inhabitants were largely unremarkable, other than one dark-skinned one whose filed teeth made him look like a vampire.

After all 21 of us had moved in and arranged our bunks in rows on either side of the wall, we took stock of our situation. The new environment depressed us all. Meals would now be delivered to the cell, so we wouldn't even be able to circulate in the prison population. Bickering began among the Americans who had opposed the demands for new conditions and those who had supported the action.

The *Jefe* began to describe how things were to be run in the cell, and it was clear that friction was going to develop quickly over his assumption of control.

In the morning, the *Jefe* handled the distribution of food; arguments about portions began almost immediately, and Lonnie badmouthed him openly. The depressing aspects of the new residence became clearer as the day wore on, especially with the realization that the trading of Swiss Red Cross packages was likely to come to a standstill.

Then the *Jefe* and Israel began walking up and down the length of the cell as if strolling through a park, arm-in-arm. Obviously, this was their custom and added to our doubts about this suspicious couple, who reminded us of the old Mutt and Jeff comic strip characters. On the first night, this scene took on a bizarre aspect. In a gesture of friendliness, one of the Americans had offered their Right Guard deodorant for the *Jefe* to spray under his arms. This was a novel experience for them. As they walked, Israel would turn his head into the Chief's armpits and sniff the fragrance of the Right Guard. As they walked along, the *Jefe* sang the lyrics to an old Turtle's tune, *So Happy Together.*

Imagine me and you, I do
I think about you day and night, it's only right
To think about the girl you love and hold her tight
So happy together

It seemed oddly ironic, given the seeds of hostility in the dank air.

The cell left everyone in bad spirits that night. Orville and Grog were almost reduced to tears with bitterness over the location change, which they had never desired. They had been happy with the status quo.

Months earlier in *Once*, I had asked Roger, who always seemed to be in good spirits, if he was ever unhappy. He said rarely, but that night in *Zona Uno*, he told me he was unhappy. We ended up talking for an hour or two that night, looking for any positive aspects of our new situation. We agreed that should an attack of dysentery occur again, it would be a lot better to have 25 people competing for two toilets than 420 going for five. Also, there would not be the constant threat of stealing like we had in *Once*. We agreed the cramped and poorly lit quarters, limits to outside parts of the prison, and our strange roommates would create a psychological challenge. Sublimated hostilities were certain to surface.

We all went to sleep early that night. Socializing offered little comfort, and I'm sure more letters were written home than usual.

The morning offered a brighter picture. We all received larger portions of *leche con café*, although an argument arose over the excessive size of the *Jefe's* portion. He insisted that his responsibilities as trustee and his longevity in the cell warranted the double serving. After challenging anyone in the cell to a fight, he realized that he was approaching the issue all wrong and that a diplomatic stance was likely to avoid future problems with his immediate neighbors. It was decided that Henn, the oldest of the prisoners, would serve the portions of food and this was generally accepted.

One of the advantages of the new cell was that we could take showers almost any time of day we wanted. A 55-gallon drum was positioned beneath the water spigot. When the water was turned on, it would fill up. Using a quart tin container, the person would douse himself with the water he dipped out of the large drum.

Since meals were brought directly to our cell, we often would not leave the dungeon for days at a time. We kept our own trays and would stand in line as Henn portioned out the food. This gave us a better opportunity to see the ingredients used in some of the food. One day Henn took his first ladleful of soup and pulled up an intact rooster claw. On other days it might be a fish head or other unappetizing membrane.

Even so, the portions were, for the most part, much better than we had gotten at *Once*.

After three nights, when we were beginning to get accustomed to the *Jefe's* ways, the Americans resumed their nightly bridge matches. Then they got on a poker kick. The second straight night of playing, the cell was raided. Three guards came bursting through the cell, overturned the makeshift table, and confiscated the cigarette "chips" and handmade cards. Everyone was certain the *Jefe* had been the stool pigeon. From that night on, he was included in the matches and the cell was never raided again. These poker games improved the relationship with the *Jefe* immeasurably; he was an avid player, reminiscent of the title character in *Sgt. Bilko,* an old TV show from the 1950s. After the first week, though, he lost his shirt in every card game he joined.

Other activities filled the time for the rest of us who were not card-playing aficionados. We began to take an interest in the sign language used by the *maricónes* to speak right in front of the unwitting guards. It was a hand alphabet for the deaf and served as an excellent opportunity to study the language since communication was at one-quarter speed and spelled out.

Now that the tensions of *Once* were lessened, I became more involved with drawing. A Spanish health book provided skeletal studies, and I began to compile a small sheaf of drawings, which I copied from the book's illustrations. When I was involved in drawing—concentrating on line quality, variations in shade, adding depth and form—my mind was in a zone without the barriers of the cell, the prison, or Havana. Time was of no dimension, and I could soar far into a liberating zone of peace. This revived the keen interest I had in architecture so long ago.

Once again I was intrigued with the design of spaces for living that were both efficient and aesthetically pleasing. I began to contemplate the application of domes for the many steep landscapes in Hawaii. I envisioned excavating into the slopes in a terraced pattern and installing tilted domes situated to be part roof and part panoramic window. It seemed to be a worthwhile solution to life on an island where many of the building materials had to be shipped in. Contemplating the stress factors on the structure and functional layout gave me hours of distraction. It was the only time since I had abandoned architecture studies that I wished I had a calculus book to study.

Others concentrated on different topics; Robert and Chet exchanged their mechanical and sailing knowledge and provided a fund of practical information.

Due to a request that I had made shortly after entering *Zona Uno*, the crew of the *Silver Sands* was summoned to the administrative office of the prison in November and permitted to retrieve a few of our personal items. For the first time in more than three months, I got to wear my glasses for nearsightedness. It was rare that I ever needed them within the confines of the cell; however, it was a big morale boost just to get familiar, personal items. I was also allowed to get my sunglasses, two large towels and a pack of American cigarettes, which I had last had at the Immigration Building in July. Chet, Dan and Cal got similar items, including other pairs of shoes.

DUNGEON DIVERSIONS: NOVEMBER 1973

Life was not entirely bleak in this netherworld, and we found ways to fill the time. At night the *maricónes* often provided a source of entertainment, performing where we could see them behind the bars of their cell door. One would wrap towels around his chest, waist and head and dance à la Carmen Miranda. With his lipstick, eye shadow and saucy walk, he was quite believable. All he needed was a fruit-laden headdress to complete the image.

The *maricónes* were the primary smugglers of items in and out of the prison. They had few qualms about using their orifices to conceal pills, marijuana and other contraband. One day one of them—a large fellow—was challenged to see if he could consume a bowl piled a foot high with spaghetti. It would be no small feat as the bowl was the size of a large salad bowl. It was hard to imagine one body containing all that pasta. Bets were placed and faces pressed against the barred windows as prisoners in all the cells tried to see the outcome. Cheers of encouragement and disbelievers shouted, "*No puede comer todo!*"

He was three-quarters finished when the guards broke up the eating exhibition, just as the betting was getting heavy. The *Jefe* had two packs riding on the *maricón* finishing the bowl of starch. The *Jefe* figured that since a week earlier this *maricón* had reportedly smuggled in three packs of cigarettes at one time, he had the internal capacity. After learning of this, we recalled with revulsion the crumpled cigarettes that were in trading circulation a week earlier, and which we had smoked.

My headaches had been continual since the jar was broken on the side of my head the day of the riot. Now they were more severe and made me highly irritable. Before, for a few minutes after waking up, I had often been a bit of a crank. But now, immediately upon waking, my skull felt like it would implode with pressure coming from all sides.

The pain subsided in an hour or two, but until it did, I was in pain and short-tempered.

Finally, it was arranged for me to go up to the prison hospital for X-rays. At about 6:30 one morning, I was called out of the cell and escorted to the staircase, which was located near the main prison entrance. At the top, I had to wait by the laboratory until an intern could be located to conduct me along the crooked path over the cells and their airshafts. From these parapets, I could look over the awakening city of Havana. It was such a change from the walls that had filled my view for the last four months. My eyes sucked in the drama of everyday life in the city—trucks hauling materials, smoke from bakeries, factories and generating stations, high-rise apartments, plazas, trees, office buildings and hotels. At another time, these sights would have seemed mundane; on this morning I just wanted to gaze at them and see life anew—the simple glory of everyday occurrences that now were so precious and rare. As unlikely as it seemed, I also wanted to make a mental picture of which direction I would go if I were to attempt an escape from the prison.

As I made my way into one of the administrative offices, I saw my first woman—dressed in a fatigue-colored blouse and skirt—in many months. Despite the length of deprivation, it did not alter my image of her: she was a cumbersome sow accessorized with a demeanor to match.

An intern arrived and took me to a walled-in section just above the dining hall in a courtyard surrounded on three sides by examination rooms, convalescent wards and medical equipment. A couple of Cuban patients gawked at me while I leaned on an airshaft and stared at their large stomach stitches.

While I was waiting for the technicians to show up, a Cuban appeared from the patient's ward, walked over, and told me there was another American there who wanted to talk to me. I walked over to the entrance of the ward as a man sitting on a lawn chair, made of continuous pipe-framing and a sheet-metal seat, crab-crawled around the corner. Both of his ankles were swollen to the size of grapefruits. He moved by extending his injured feet and lurching the chair forward. His first words were to bum a cigarette. I rolled one from my sparse supply and gave it to him. I asked him who he was and why he was in prison.

"I'm Louis," he replied with a trailing whine of disbelief. "Three of us came here with $2 million and *they put us in prison!*"

He sounded as if his astonishment at such treatment had not diminished during the year he had been in captivity. My mind went back to newspaper accounts of the hijacking he was referring to. I recalled that three Black men from Detroit—two of them brothers and suspects in the killing of a police officer—had boarded a commercial flight. As soon as the plane was in the air, they had produced pistols and began to commandeer the aircraft. Then they flew all over—to Canada then to Tennessee where they threatened to crash the jetliner into a Tennessee Valley Authority dam if their demands for money were not met. Finally, after obtaining the millions in cash, they flew to Cuba, expecting to be greeted with open arms. When the story of the hijacking was on the evening news back in the States,

I recalled that one of the mysteries of the hijacking was how the perpetrators had gotten their guns past security. Thinking it might be useful to authorities when I returned home, I asked Louis how they had snuck their guns on board. Louis told me they had made no exceptional efforts to sneak the guns on when they boarded, but rather that security was lax.

Weeks earlier I had heard along the prison grapevine that a hijacker was moved to the hospital at *Príncipe* after an ill-fated escape attempt. I asked Louis what had happened. He told me that the three men who had hijacked the plane had found their way out through air ducts at *La Cabaña*. They crawled across the walls, and would, more than likely, have had their freedom were it not for the 20-foot jump across and down the other side of the moat. Two of the three made it safely; the hapless Louis did not. He landed hard and broke both of his ankles. Witnessing his extreme pain, the other two ended up going down and carrying him to the main entrance where they had to bang on the gates to get back inside.

Before our conversation went any further, I was summoned into the X-ray room.

They took pictures of my skull, front and side. Then I waited in the courtyard again for an escort back down to *Zona Uno*. Seven political prisoners were brought by as I waited and came right over to me. They looked almost distinguished in their immaculately pressed yellow uniforms. Each had a bearing that set them apart from the common criminal in the general prison population with which I had become familiar. A 27-year-old Black member of their group asked in precise English who I was and how long I had been in Cuba. I explained as briefly as I could and told him I'd been there six months. He then asked, "What?" In my excitement, I had failed to realize that English was his second language and had rambled on without articulating properly. I repeated my words more slowly and eliminated much of my usual slang; he then interpreted for the rest of the group.

I asked him how long he had been in captivity, and he replied that he had been in prison since he was 19 and had learned all his English while in captivity.

Knowing I was going to be summoned away at any moment made it difficult to carry on a meaningful conversation with these men who had sacrificed their freedom for their principles.

The intern appeared and I was hustled off, thinking the whole way of that group of impressive men, with whom I had just had a few precious moments. While I was being held due to my own questionable acts, they were there for their convictions.

Upon returning to the cell, I was besieged with questions about what it was like in the hospital and what the political prisoners were like. I then found out that the hospital facilities at *Príncipe* were much better than anything at *El Morro* and *La Cabaña* and the political prisoners and hijackers confined there came to *Príncipe* frequently for short periods of treatment.

The prison official in charge of our cell and section was far more responsive to our requests than the one we had at *Once*. He had been instrumental in seeing that I had gotten my glasses and other items. He now arranged for us to get out in the small courtyard immediately outside our cell. Usually, we could get out of the cell once or twice a week for two hours. We would meander about, look at the narrow patch of sky framed by the 20-foot-high walls, and wistfully watch the clouds drift by. Flies were prevalent in the bright sunlight and always provided an annoying distraction, though, I observed with curiosity, this type did not seem to bite.

Before one such session in the courtyard, I had observed an intern flushing the ears of some of the inmates with a syringe with the needle removed. My ears always had been subject to frequent infections and had been bothering me recently. I asked the intern if he would be able to improve my hearing as my ear canal seemed to be slightly obstructed and a mild jet of water might dislodge it. I sat in a chair and held a basin, which caught the gushing overflow. My left ear felt much better after it was flushed. Then he went to the right ear. For an unknown reason, he pressed the plunger on the syringe with such force that the jet of fluid nearly knocked me off the chair as I cried out in pain. He had practically slammed his hand down on the plunger and had torn my eardrum.

From that point on, I had perhaps 50 percent of my hearing, except when I yawned and the torn edges of the membrane mated enough to vibrate to conduct sound. It significantly added to my isolation and misery in the dungeon. Between the headache, loss of hearing, poor diet, uncertain future and dingy cell frequently filled with dissension, my life was at an all-time low. My fears about my family continued to grow: were my parents okay, had I disappointed them, could I ever face them again without shame?

By now, late November, we could hear sounds late into the night as the larger prison population was being relocated to work in the fields for the *zafra*, the sugar cane harvest. Though this involved backbreaking labor, the prisoners eagerly awaited the improved diet they would soon receive. Their work would also reduce their sentences. In time, the prison population would be cut from about 6,000 inmates to fewer than 1,000. With the change in numbers came the rumor that *Príncipe* was in its final days as a prison and was about to be turned into a museum. Like all rumors, we took those with a grain of salt. The change in prison numbers brought us larger portions of food, though, and on some days, we were given more than we could eat.

When not with Chet and Dan, I spent most of my time associating with Richard and Roger. The Cubans had captured Richard when he was 21 and in many ways, he was like an impressionable teen, frozen in adolescence. At that time, he probably thought he was taking on big responsibilities and on the way to becoming a wealthy pot dealer. He was on the threshold of making many of the discoveries, both good and bad, that normal life brings to most people at that age. His deepening awareness of women had just begun—in fact may have been the reason he was compelled to become a smuggler—when it was abruptly halted. We talked about this a lot.

Richard joined the Navy right out of high school but had trouble adjusting to the hierarchy and discipline and was discharged when he deliberately placed a joint on an officer's desk. Once a civilian again, he got into selling grass; eventually, he escalated his operation by getting into the actual importing.

Roger was drafted into the Army shortly after he was married, served in a combat unit in Vietnam and saw service in Hue during the Tet Offensive of 1968. He was honorably discharged but returned a changed man. He was nothing like the one who had been married before the war and his marriage broke up almost immediately upon his return. After the war, he lost interest in the lifestyle that his affluent and influential parents had assumed he would follow, instead he was drawn to old friends who had become part of the hippie counterculture in his absence. He became more involved with marijuana and then with LSD. He became a vegetarian and for a summer lived in a teepee in the mountains.

Although I had met many people who had used LSD, and a few of them said they had adverse effects from their experiences, Roger appeared to have had an entirely different experience. His consumption of acid, though quite frequent, had usually been preceded by a three-day fast. He approached the use of such a potent substance with a sacred respect. He also only used the highest quality LSD. He told me that at one time he was involved in the sale of large quantities—sometimes in lots as large as 1,000 hits—of Owsley Acid, LSD that was so popular it was informally trademarked with a variety of imprints, including Disney characters and images of Alice in Wonderland.

Roger maintained with some pride that the LSD he had sold had all been "Orange Sunshine," one source removed from the manufacturer.

While in prison, Roger had relented somewhat in his vegetarian diet. I asked him how he decided what was appropriate to eat.

"If it can run away from me, I don't eat it," was his simple reply.

While in *Príncipe*, however, he began to eat fish since the sources of protein were scant. Curiously, he often gave away sizable portions of his food, but he was the only American to put on weight—except Jay and Burris who seemed to be constantly eating or bartering for food with items from their Swiss packs.

Roger was generally silent and often meditated for long periods. Whenever disputes arose among the Americans, he was one of the last to speak; when he did, however, everyone paid attention. I never saw him do anything unfair, and his example made me try harder to cope with my upsetting circumstances.

Roger also stimulated my interest in the *I Ching: The Book of Changes*. He had consulted the *I Ching*, which provided an oracle by tossing coins to get a hexagram, shortly before leaving Colombia with Will and Jeff. He was warned of the negative changes that were to take place.

All the while, I continued to have problems with my ear. After weeks of waiting, I was finally scheduled to have my ear looked at by Dr. Cardinoche, Richard's friend from his time in the rooftop prison hospital. The 70-year-old doctor was serving a life sentence for transmitting information to U.S. intelligence agencies. He had 16 honorary degrees from American medical schools for his outstanding work in several special fields of medicine, including plastic surgery. It was reassuring to know that such an esteemed man was to treat me for my still undiagnosed problem. Richard accompanied me up to the hospital where he would act as my interpreter. It was nice to get out of the cell that morning, as dissension in there was particularly strong.

The friction had come about because I did not want Lonnie to accompany me. Experience had taught me that Lonnie would, more than likely, utilize the opportunity to try to get prescription drugs for a binge party. In doing so, the medical purpose of the trip to the hospital would be neglected.

I put a lot of importance on getting good medical attention—especially since it was my head that was malfunctioning. When I had chosen Richard as my interpreter, Lonnie became belligerent, and Chet sided with him. They remained in the cell with little opportunity to properly let off steam, which only compounded the problem, particularly since there was no private place there to withdraw.

Once at the hospital, Richard explained my problem to Dr. Cardinoche and then introduced me. The doctor examined the afflicted ear with a funnel and called Richard over to look. Richard noted that he could see the bone behind my eardrum—not the best news I had heard that day. I was told to keep the ear dry and was given prescription drops after the doctor cleaned it out.

While awaiting our escort for the return trip downstairs, we went over to the patients' ward and met a man identified as Raphael del Pine. He had been a friend of Castro's in college, but after Fidel's takeover, Raphael had opposed him. He was flying a small plane over Cuba dropping leaflets when he was shot down and seriously injured. He had been in prison for 11 years and told us about the hunger strike he sustained for 30 days. At that time Fidel had visited him personally and granted some of his demands, one of which was that he be permitted to call home to Miami once a year. He was a fascinating man, and I would have liked to have visited longer.

On the way back to our cell, we were surprised to see Jeff. A few weeks before the riot he had been moved up to the hospital because of a blotchy skin ailment. We quickly brought him up to date on the news from downstairs and he promised to drop some pills and messages down our airshaft.

Several times after that, Jeff would yell down the airshaft to give us bulletins on the information that traveled faster upstairs due to the movement of prisoners from other facilities. He had heard all kinds of indications that Cuba-U.S. relations were improving, and we might be released soon as a political gesture or peace offering.

On the morning of December 17, 1973, we were startled to learn that we would be moving within the hour. Everyone wondered whether the rumor was true and if we were being moved to the new prison or to *La Cabaña*. We were told to leave our mattresses, which reinforced the idea that we were being moved to the new "deluxe" prison. Soon everyone had their bags crammed full of their belongings: cigarette packs, vitamins, playing cards, books, stamps and stationery, cups and spoons, toiletries and spare clothing. For the first time in two months, we left the dungeon that we had called home.

TRIBUNAL: DECEMBER 23, 1973

Then we were led *away* from the prison entrance. This had not been expected. I felt like a nomadic merchant to the East with a destination unknown as we trudged through the gates to the courtyard that ran along the mess hall. We continued to the gate at the other end and past another narrower courtyard directly into a cell, which previously had been occupied by the elderly inmates and seemed immense compared to the dank dungeon that was *Zona Uno*.

These new accommodations were far better than our earlier confined settings. Two large, barred openings straddled the cell entrance, permitting a significant amount of light in. The walls were whitewashed, which gave the cell a certain luxurious atmosphere. The barrel-vaulted cell was almost 100 feet long and at least 40 feet wide. On either side of a large aisle were neat rows of beds with clean mattresses, and a separate room was located to the right. A genuine lidless toilet was inside—something none of us had seen for five months. It lacked the traditional wood-hinged seat, but no one seemed to care. It was a welcome change from the squat, block-style latrines we had grown accustomed to and which had always aggravated my bad knee.

Adjacent to the john was a small shower section with two 55-gallon drums. One of them had a steam exhaust pipe leading into it from the kitchen. We became accustomed to the early morning gurgling bubbles of steam ascending to the surface of the drum that would heat the water to almost boiling, retaining the heat until late at night.

Showers consisted of pouring a proportionate amount of cold water into a quart container and then raising the temperature by dipping it into the steam-heated drum. This was a luxury—uncommon throughout all of Cuba's prisons—a hot shower.

We began to rearrange the beds in the cell, continuing to collect ourselves in groups that were for the most part, amicable. As none of the beds were stacked like bunks, the large cell seemed even more spacious. Everyone's spirits were uplifted by our new, "plush" surroundings. Food was still served in the cell, but at least now we could see well enough to identify what we were eating and could spot the rocks and foreign particles which frequently "seasoned" the food and caused chipped teeth.

On the evening of our arrival, the crew of the *Silver Sands* was summoned to the administration section of the prison. As we walked across the star courtyard, we could see how much of the prison had been vacated. A few hundred now occupied what had reportedly held 6,000 inmates just a month or two earlier. It seemed eerily deserted compared to the crowded days of August.

As soon as we reached the administration rooms, Chet was summoned into an office and was inside for an hour. When he returned, he confirmed our developing suspicions: we were to go to trial the following day. Cal, and then Dan, were called in separately. Meanwhile, Chet and I discussed what had transpired during his meeting.

Chet said he had been told that in the morning we would go before *Revoluntionario Tribunal Numero Uno*—the highest court in Cuba. A man we had never seen or talked to before, who identified himself only as the Captain, would conduct the meeting with the four of us through an interpreter. Chet had been told that if we failed to cooperate with our prosecution in any way, new charges would be added during the trial, and we might face a sentence of 30 years.

My hopes for an early and imminent release dropped. He said he had tried arguing with the Captain during the questioning but had been met with threats of further charges even before the trial began. As it was, we were to be charged with smuggling marijuana and illegal entry into Cuban territorial waters.

I was finally called in for the interview. The Captain was a thin, short man in his early 30s. He had a shock of dark hair that continually fell over his forehead as he talked animatedly and assertively through the interpreter in a brisk and commanding manner. He reminded me of a rat with his predominant top front teeth and sharp features. The interpreter was in his early 50s, gray-haired, bespectacled and articulate. *He* reminded me of a college professor and seemed urbane and kind. Since he was not introduced, in my mind I gave him the name of Professor. I felt that at another time, under different circumstances, we would have had a pleasant conversation, conveying tidbits of knowledge in a collegial way.

The Professor translated simultaneously as the words were being spoken, and I marveled that he could both hear in one language and translate it to the other at each moment. From his expressions, I had the distinct impression he disliked the contents of the Spanish he had to translate for our benefit—perhaps it was just the difficulty of listening and conversing at the same time.

The Captain began by stating we were to go to trial the following morning. He explained that there were only two things that we could possibly have been doing in Cuban waters: smuggling drugs or committing an aggressive act against the Cuban people. To make things "easier" on us, he and his superiors had decided only to prosecute us for smuggling, which would carry a minimal penalty. The other charges could result in our being shot by a firing squad or as much as 30 years in prison. The world had turned into a bad play with no audience, no stage exits and no happy ending in sight.

When I began to protest, he crushed any opposition saying that further charges would be added if we did not cooperate fully in his prosecution. Chet had warned me about this, so I let the whole thing pass as hopeless. The Captain then asked a few biographical questions. Had I ever been in the military? Where was I working immediately before working on the boat? What was my experience as a navigator? Then I was dismissed. The whole thing took less than 20 minutes. In closing, I asked if representatives of our government would be present to witness the proceedings. He said the Swiss Embassy officials would be observers.

We were downcast as we went over the proceedings of the intimidating meeting on the walk back to the cell.

Of all the Americans in *Príncipe*, Lonnie was the only one to have appeared before *Tribunal Numero Uno*, and he questioned us thoroughly about what had happened. He thought it was highly favorable that we weren't being tried as common criminals as all the smugglers had. He told us that, although *Numero Uno* could change and add charges during the trials, they also were more likely to reconsider any sentence they might impose and reduce it. He also believed it meant they had to go beyond the outstanding laws to prosecute us. He believed that our only hope was to completely deny everything the Cubans wanted us to admit or agree to. The options were hardly encouraging to consider: cooperate and face four years of imprisonment or stand up to the prosecution's plans and face 30 years of confinement.

Cal, Dan, Chet and I stayed up late into the night trying to figure out what to do. Whatever we decided, we had to be united and speak with one voice. Long after midnight, we agreed that we would sleep on it and make a commitment in the morning and went to sleep wondering what the next day would bring. But we had not reached a conclusion. It was a restless night knowing that the events of the following day would determine the rest of our lives.

We were awakened at sunrise and told we had 45 minutes to get ready for our departure for court. We huddled together and took a collective deep breath. What would we do?

We decided to fight and deny all the charges. Our unity was a source of optimism. Like a team coming out of a locker room at half-time, with the score favoring the other team, we felt solidarity like we had not had since our vessel had been impounded.

We were conducted to the prison gates and placed in an *aula.* Our mood brightened during the half-hour ride. The decision was behind us and we were resolved. Some of the scenery toward the end of the trip looked familiar, and we realized we were not far from *La Cabaña.*

This postcard shows *El Morro* at the entrance to the Havana harbor. *El Morro* was used to hold political prisoners and was adjacent to *La Cabaña,* the citadel, where we stayed for only two days. Our trial before the *Revoluntionario Tribunal Numero Uno* was held in the little building to the right.

Finally, the jail-on-wheels lurched to a stop. As we exited, we were surprised to see the frothy, glistening waves of the harbor on our left; across it was the entire city of Havana. I felt a burst of joy as I could look out from the mouth of the harbor to the open sea; *El Morro* and its lighthouse rose high on a cliff to our right. This in itself was not reassuring because we had been told that executions were carried out in its courtyard.

I breathed in the salt air, pulling in the wonderful, scrubbed breeze coming off the water for just a few moments and I longed to be on a vessel plying its way north.

We were led to a concrete building with a wooden roof, partially concealed by trees and large ferns. As we walked toward it, we saw the enormous cannons, which at one time must have been vital to the security of the port, but now were mere massive showpieces. A dozen or more military personnel in drab olive uniforms were occupied with chores, passing the time or taking in the sight of the foreigners about to go on trial. Once again, I felt like a zoo animal.

Once inside, we saw the Captain again. I felt a degree of friendliness with the Professor, who I assumed would be translating during the trial. The Captain engaged in a short conversation with Chet who asked who was going to represent us and if we could talk to him before the trial. The Captain replied through the Professor that he would "try to arrange it."

A few minutes later, we were conducted to a table in another room, behind which sat a heavyset Black man in his early 40s who was introduced as our counsel.

Chet asked him if we could see a copy of the law under which we were being prosecuted. Our counsel replied that he had no copy of the law with him, but that it was known as the Law of the Sierra Maestra. He did not ask us how we intended to plea, but he did ask us our ages and our professions. He offered nothing in the way of advice but cautioned us that other charges could be added. In that undefined space between two strangers where they try to assess each other, despite the absence of a history or word of mouth, I felt an intuitive inkling that he would try to look out for our best interests. I was struck by the possibility that his welfare might be jeopardized by *too* good a defense of our case.

We were led into a small room that looked as if it had been a chapel at one time, with 10 rows of high-backed pews separated by a center aisle. Each of the pews seated four people and faced two desks for the prosecutor, the Professor, the defense counsel and the stenographer. The desks were placed in front of a long, low dais with a massive wooden podium and three heavily upholstered, high-backed chairs. Light entered through a large open window filled with large leafy plants.

We were instructed to sit in the front pews and those behind us began to fill with men in drab olive uniforms. Immediately outside this courtroom, we observed three men in suits silhouetted in the doorway. Chet went to the Captain and asked if they were the Swiss Embassy officials. The Captain said yes and allowed us to talk with them.

Chet walked over and introduced himself as the captain of our boat and asked how they were planning to defend us as agents of our government. They looked at each other, somewhat taken aback by what they seemed to consider a strange request. At least one became visibly nervous. They indicated they were merely observers who would report the events of the proceedings back to the U.S. State Department and ensure no irregularities took place. Chet began to tell them we had been held incommunicado, had had no opportunity to prepare a legal defense, and were being charged unfairly and under duress. They patronizingly replied that they would do all they could to help us and would see that the State Department was informed of anything significant. They underscored that they had no strong position from which to act on our behalf with the Cuban authorities. But Chet put them on notice that this was not an open-and-shut case of smuggling. Apparently, they thought their appearance was *pro forma*, just as it had been for all the smugglers and hijackers we had met.

We returned to our seats. By now the small room was filled with soldiers, both male and female. There were two other men in business suits besides the Swiss, but they seemed to have no affiliation with them. The Captain and defense attorney then entered, and now it became clear that the Captain was the prosecuting attorney. We felt we had been deceived the previous night as he had never identified himself as such. Within a few minutes, three men seated themselves behind the massive counter. We were about to begin.

The Captain began by rising from his chair, saluting the revolution and tribunal heads and closing with the revolution's slogan, "*Libertad o Muerte*"—Liberty or Death. He then grandiosely removed his gun belt with holstered sidearm and began to state the charges against us. He called his first and only witness, Captain Rodriguez.

Rodriguez was asked how far we had come into Cuban waters. He replied that we were within 1.7 miles of shore when the gunboat boarded us. To me, that did not sound all that hard to believe. We had been very close. Rodriguez then produced a sheaf of photographs depicting the equipment found on our boat during the seizure. They showed Chet's pistol and .22 rifle, my explosives case, ammo boxes, LORAN, Buck knives, sheathed knives, radios, headphones and serial numbers of various pieces of equipment. He described our rope-cutting knives as being "commando" knives and our rafts as being identical to those used by the CIA in their assaults on Cuba. He went on to state that we were on our way to Jamaica to pick up marijuana when the alert Cuban gunboat spotted us. His statement, with occasional prodding from the Captain, lasted one hour.

The defense attorney then asked Rodriguez one or two feeble questions, such as if we had fired upon the gunboat when it approached, or had we offered any resistance. He replied that we had not and left the witness chair.

Chet was then called. Standing before the Tribunal, he attempted to give his responses to the questions put to him by the prosecutor, who frequently interrupted Chet's replies with further questions. His initial questions were primarily biographical: where he was from, his age, military service, and his experience with boats. He then asked Chet if he had been involved in the smuggling of marijuana.

"No," Chet replied.

I thought my heart would stop in that instant. From that moment on, we had set our course for the trial. Could we stick to it?

Instantly the Captain's face turned from surprise to anger—he was mentally agile and was on to us: despite his use of fear tactics the preceding evening, we weren't playing along with the script he had in mind. But he was taken aback and unprepared. It was as if he had not done his homework, thinking it was going to be an easy textbook trial.

He dismissed Chet prematurely, thinking he would gain his objective with one of the less bold crew members. He called Dan forward.

After a few routine biographical questions, the prosecutor began touching upon the objectives of our voyage, laying out his questions in such a fashion that all Dan had to do was answer affirmatively. He didn't. The Captain nearly exploded, losing a substantial amount of control. He began to call Dan a liar. No objections were heard from our defense attorney. He then began to paint exact details of how we were to go to Jamaica to smuggle marijuana. Dan continued to deny that our cruise was motivated by any other reason than to test out the vessel, which had presented us with ongoing navigation problems. The Captain also interrupted him frequently. The fact that he had to go through an interpreter was further handicapping him from using a staccato of questions designed to fool or confound the witnesses.

He kept Dan on the stand for almost two hours. Toward the end of the examination, he began to point to the fact that neither Dan nor Chet had served in the regular military. I began to see the new tactic he was developing. Then I was struck by the irony that none of the crew of the *Silver Sands* had served in the military. He would try to make it an obvious assumption that we were all employed in another capacity which exempted us from compulsory military service. Finally, Dan was dismissed from the prosecutor's arduous examination. The defense attorney asked Dan how old he was and if he had ever worked for the U.S. government. Dan replied he was 24 and had not seen military service.

The Tribunal then recessed for lunch for an hour and a half. As we stood up to stretch our legs, I noticed that the entire audience was either mulatto or Hispanic. The only Black in the room was our counsel. What the significance of this was, I didn't know, but it struck me as being an odd coincidence.

The hours of questions and anxiety left us all with a common urge. Upon request, we were conducted to urinals located a short distance away from the courtroom.

Afterward, we shared our impressions of the proceedings. We had no idea of how it all looked to the Swiss, but we had no doubts that the prosecutor was displeased by the way things were going. We expected him to pull out all the stops when he had collected himself and the Tribunal resumed. We spent the remainder of the lunch recess in a state of passive anxiety. We were not offered any food.

Cal was summoned first when the Tribunal reconvened. Surprisingly, the prosecutor did not begin with a full-scale, aggressive cross-examination. His questions were similar to those that had been asked before lunch, and the audience quickly began to fall into the post-lunch doldrums. Even the three presiding Tribunal judges were drifting off—one or two of them might have been sleeping. They barely moved for extended periods and at times closed their eyes as though considering nuances of the law.

All of a sudden, the prosecutor wheeled around from his cross-examining posture, pointed a finger at Dan, and accused him of insulting the Tribunal and the Revolution with one of his gestures. I looked toward Dan, and he looked back at me as if to say, "I don't know what he's talking about." If nothing else, the onlookers were startled by the change in rhetoric and became more attentive. It seemed to be merely a theatrical ploy to sustain interest and unnerve us.

Finally, by late afternoon, it was my turn. If not for my resolve, I thought I would be an unconvincing failure. This situation and the welfare of my crewmates required me to lie, not something that came easily to me. I stood and took center stage, now more a member of the cast than of a crew.

I was asked for the same biographical data, then posed more specific questions regarding my training and experience as a navigator. The questions then became more pointed.

How had we managed to get clearance to leave U.S. waters? My attempts to explain that no clearance was necessary were cut short by several questions about the reasons I had not served in the regular U.S. military service. I explained that when I tried to enlist in the Navy, a blood test had rendered me ineligible for service, except during a major call-up of servicemen; then I had drawn a high number in the draft lottery. The Captain dismissed my medical explanations as further lies. Then he began to phrase his queries so that they were more statements than questions. He had completely abandoned his questions tying us to a smuggling operation and now was accusing us of attempting a raid on the Cuban coastline, right where previous "imperialistic acts of aggression" had taken place.

During his tirade, it began to rain and the whole experience became even more surreal. I looked through the window beyond the Tribunal and watched the rain glistening off the ferns. The whole world seemed to be crying. Had everything in my life been leading up to this otherworldly moment?

I was excused and the prosecutor began his two-hour summation. His scathing rhetoric began with calling us liars, typical of the Capitalist system. We were part and parcel of the oppressive system, which had caused illiteracy, poverty and prostitution in Cuba before Fidel Castro had thrown off the yoke of imperialism. He even blamed us for smoking up most of his cigarettes the previous evening during his questioning. I thought he was now relying on oratory rather than facts to support the accusations. As he ranted, I noticed a pained expression sweep over the Professor's face when the prosecutor's tone, volume and inflection became most dramatic and damning. I felt sorry for him, convinced that he had to convey sentiments he didn't share.

It was dark by the time the prosecutor concluded his oratory. He closed by adding that we should be given additional charges and a total sentence of ten years.

The defense attorney then began his brief summation. He pointed out that it was a basic tenant of justice in any system that guilt must be proven. He stated that no such proof had been presented and therefore we were innocent and deserved the restoration of our freedom. He was done in less than two minutes.

The trial was over. Although it was probably the most dramatic day of my life, it ended without a decision. We would not know the verdict that day.

The courtroom emptied quickly. Chet was allowed to confer with the Swiss and he asked them if they would now do something on our behalf. They appeared optimistic, for this was apparently one of the few opportunities they had had in recent years to work on a case in which the Americans had not been involved in a blatant violation of international law or caught with evidence of drugs.

Chet asked the Swiss if they would send this message to the U.S. State Department: We had been placed under duress during most of our confinement in Cuba, and we had not been involved in any illegal activity at the time of our seizure. The Swiss agreed and gave Chet almost a full pack of cigarettes, which we enjoyed on the long ride back to *Príncipe.*

Our mood during our return was one of relief—almost jubilation. We each felt that we had done the right thing by taking a stand against the Cubans.

Whether it would bring us freedom in the days ahead, only time would tell. But for the moment, we had worked together as a team, and the fetid fear and doubts that had accumulated and clung to us the last seven months had lifted.

GOODBYES: DECEMBER 24, 1973

When we returned to *Príncipe* less than an hour later, we were placed in the holding cell and given our first food since *desayuno*. The portions were large and we ate heartily. Our mood was almost joyous and the relief from the day's tensions liberated our spirits. We knew we had taken a great risk and, for that day, we had solidarity.

As we entered our new home cell, the other Americans clustered around us to learn how things had gone. We were the big news of the day. Several of them had advised us not to buck the Cuban prosecution; now they seemed almost ashamed for having said so. Lonnie was elated that we had fouled the Cubans' attempts to have us take their bait.

The following day we were still talking about the trial when Jeff, who was standing in the courtyard of the hospital immediately overhead, yelled to us. He had heard of our move the previous day, so he dropped some drugs down through one of the two airshafts. This time Jeff dropped down a few Darvons, a mild painkiller. These were usually saved for a Saturday night "party" and were comparable to a few slugs of bourbon.

The days in the new cell were like a vacation in comparison to the old cell, and we were allowed out into the courtyard for several hours a day. The baker's cells were located nearby, and they would frequently bring in large rolls made with oil and eggs, unlike the standard prison fare made from water, yeast and flour. Chet and Dan began to jog regularly in the immense cell. Chet said he was getting in shape to go home. I secretly harbored the belief that we would not be in Cuba much longer, but I could not ascribe it to any rational thinking. The days held hope and felt brighter.

December 21st arrived and along with it, a letter from my mother. Although it was the first communication I had from her since I was in Florida in May, the number on the letter indicated she had sent two previously. I felt my mother's presence on the page. Because of her stroke, it was written with her left hand; her once beautiful flowing right-handed script now had a backward tilt with curves that seemed crushed into angles. It was a reminder of the life she was living as a stroke victim and the struggles this determined woman had been living with for the last three years.

November 15, 1973

Dear Gordon,

Think of you constantly. Wish we could receive a word or two from you.

Guess you know of the fuel shortage (the October Arab-Israeli War of 1973 had led to a shortage of oil). Wonder if this will affect our going to Florida next month and our return in the spring. Hope for Dad's sake it doesn't.

By the way—today is supposed to be his last day of work for the Boro of Lavallette.

They are planning a farewell dinner for him close to his retirement date 7-1-74.

How is the weather in Cuba? I understand Cuba is a beautiful island. Are you able to see any of it?

Your car insurance has run out so get in touch with us if you want us to get it covered again when you return.

How is Chet? How are you? Do you like Cuban food? What are you looking forward to having when you return?

Both Barb & Penny (friends from Honolulu) wrote when they heard where you are. Hope you are released soon. It's been a long time.

Love, Mom

Her letter was filled with irony. She always wanted to travel the world, but her trip to California to see her father as a young adult, two trips to Canada and another to Hawaii and Florida were the farthest she got from her lifetime in New Jersey. The news that my father had retired from his job that day had never been discussed before my confinement in Cuba. Guilt filled me as I was reminded of my father's need for help; perhaps the strain of my circumstances was taking a toll. Many people relied on him in his job, and he carried significant responsibility. That, plus taking care of my mother and worrying about me, must have been a big burden. I felt that all I had ever done was increase problems for him and my mother, rather than diminish them. As I recalled the years of nurturing they had provided and the countless times they had both given selflessly for me, tears filled my eyes. I went to a lonely part of the cell and stayed there in the darkness for hours. In that quiet place, apart from the rest of the world and light years from home, I resolved to never disappoint my parents again, to be a son they could be proud of, and to forever be a better human being.

The days after the trial passed with no news. We wondered when the verdict from the Tribunal would be returned. It had not been decided that day in the chapel and undoubtedly, was being decided by figures with authority greater than those who had been present for the proceedings. The Americans who had been to *Revolucionario Tribunal Numero Tres* had waited as long as eight months to get their verdicts and 4-year sentences. We heard rumors that the judicial system in

Cuba was in the process of being revamped, and outcomes and formal dispositions were to be made known within two weeks. Everything was rumor and raw speculation.

By now many of the Americans had begun to grow beards or moustaches. The section official frowned on these, but he knew he would create a bigger problem by forcibly shaving us. He let it go, but constantly cajoled us about it, sometimes even making token bribes—such as larger portions of food or books—so that we would shave and keep our hair short. Our only concession was to keep our hair trimmed, which, given the absence of shampoo and low-quality soap, was an easy decision to make.

As the prison population diminished, the rats, which filled *Príncipe's* sewers, became bolder as the food supply also diminished. At night, from the door of the cell looking toward the pile of rubbish discarded from the mess hall kitchen, we could often see as many as a dozen of the furry, chattering vermin at a time. On one occasion, a rat ran into the cell and was chased about until Cal killed him with a mighty blow from the mop. Just days before, we had adopted a black cat that had roamed by two days earlier. We named her *Medianoche* for her midnight coloring. She kept us awake during the night snapping the rat's bones and tearing its flesh. By morning, all that was left was the rat's head and two inches of its tail.

Sometimes we would get current copies of *Granma,* Cuba's national paper, which was helpful in studying Spanish vocabulary and verb tenses, even if it was not generally newsworthy. But we did learn of big changes in the States. News accounts from a month earlier astonished us when we learned of Vice President Spiro Agnew's resignation.

Now the reports of conditions in the U.S. were more alarming. The energy crisis seemed to have reached the point of desperation; daily accounts detailed how Americans spent hours in the cold to get two dollars of gas. The Cuban papers attributed this to the decline of the U.S. and our alliance with Zionist Israel. Richard translated the more delicate passages regarding the development of the Watergate investigation. Due to the slanted news coverage, the changing events, our language difficulties, and the intermittent availability of newspapers, it was difficult to tell what was really going on at home. At best, it sounded bad.

On December 24, 1973, the numbers of prisoners in our cell were called out. The three Cubans who had remained with us for the better part of the last two months were summoned. The *Jefe*, Nino, and another Cuban we called Juan Quin Quin left our cell, never to be seen or heard from again. Shortly thereafter, Lonnie discovered he had had a pack of cigarettes and a few personal items ripped off. There was little doubt that it could be anyone but the *Jefe*. This was more an act of revenge, we felt, than pure theft. The *Jefe* and Lonnie had not gotten along since we first moved into *Zona Uno*. Lonnie, of course, was furious that the Chief had gotten the last blow in.

Three hours later more numbers were called out. All the Americans who were in *Once* when we first arrived were on the list. There was a sense of alarm and hopelessness. It seemed that dramatic events were playing out in quick succession.

Our friends began packing their belongings. Where they were headed was anyone's guess. We helped them pack and carried their bags to *Príncipe's* front gate, exchanging addresses the whole way. It was understood that we would contact each other's families whenever any of us got out and try to reassure them. I waved goodbye to Richard and Roger with great sadness. They had both made the difficult times easier; Roger's example helped me put the uncertain events in a perspective that I could handle.

We returned to our cell, now an empty and cold cavern. Christmas Eve would lack even the slight warmth I had anticipated with my former cellmates.

KILLING TIME: DECEMBER 25, 1973

There was little to celebrate on Christmas Day. Our closest acquaintances had moved to places unknown. There were now only seven of us occupying the cell, which formerly had contained hundreds. We all drank a little alcohol—loaded cough syrup that contained a tiny amount of Phenobarbital—hardly a suitable substitute for the Courvoisier V.S.O.P. cognac with which I had celebrated Christmas only one year before.

The crew of the *Breeze Dream,* consisting of Robert, David and Davis, joined our group in piling the mattresses from several beds on top of one another to create a lounge. We spent Christmas lying about, sharing happy stories—outrageous things we had done or witnessed, adventures we had read or heard of, fond memories—and smoking, collectively, two or three cigarettes. No one dwelled too much on thoughts of home for the holidays as it only brought on sorrow and painful longing.

Our discussions covered almost every topic from the merits of Jamaican rum to the meaning of Jim Morrison's poem, *Horse Latitudes* on a Doors album. I was impressed that Chet could recall all the lines.

The poem had always puzzled me, but Chet explained that the Horse Latitudes referred to the currents that served as shipping lanes and used to bring horses and other vital supplies to the New World. Often, though, being so close to the Equator, the trade winds were stilled and sailing vessels were stuck in the doldrums, with no wind for propulsion. The listless vessels would rock gently, and their rigging would creak until crews were driven close to insanity. In some cases, ships would drift into the seaweed-choked Sargasso Sea. When the water was running low, and the wind extremely light, horses were pushed overboard. Years later, I learned that the first four lines of the poem had not been composed by Morrison, but rather by Nostradamus centuries earlier.

During the evening, I stood for a while at the cell door and engaged in a short conversation with one of the night guards. I mentioned that it was Christmas. The 18-year-old guard seemed to consider it just another night. We knew this particular guard as *El Rojo*—The Red—because he was an avowed Communist who had already petitioned for membership in the party. He was the only fervent Communist that I met during my entire time in Cuba.

With few diverse activities or special events, the days blurred. Living in such close quarters, with no real opportunities to get away from one another, animosities began to develop. Davis, who had been labeled "The Louie" due to his military demeanor and former rank as a lieutenant in the U.S. Army, was at the bottom of the pecking order. He had an innate talent for turning any subject—no matter how fascinating or enlightening—into an utter bore, presenting himself as an authority in almost any field. He clung tenaciously to a point of view, despite the weakness of his supporting arguments. Hostilities flared up after it was learned that he had withheld coffee that had been given to him for all of us.

There was some relief, though. On January 2, I received a letter from my best friend, Andy. He and I were exceptionally close, more like brothers than friends. We had gone to school together from the second grade on, all the way from a five-room schoolhouse in tiny Lavallette to a nearby high school. In the fourth grade, we discovered that we were born on the same day, which created a special bond. Andy was just three hours older. We had the same classes and worked together as lifeguards. We had shouldered bushel bags of clams on the decks of Point Pleasant-based commercial clamming boats that went to sea out of the Manasquan Inlet. We had even dated each other's girlfriends on two occasions. We could almost communicate by ESP and were able to express ourselves in a shorthand that bewildered many onlookers.

His letter was reassuring—for the most part. I knew he would not sugarcoat the situation, and he gave me insight into how my parents were experiencing the events of the previous eight months.

December 8, 1973, posted Dec. 12

Lavallette, NJ, USA

Gordon,

First off, I want you to know that I was enormously relieved when informed at last that you are alive and in good health. For months I had been in the dark, having virtually no idea whether you were still among the living or, if you were, what state of mind and body you were in. Secondly, I feel you should know that your mother and father are holding up solidly during this "crisis." I feel that you should hear this from me since you may feel that it would not be entirely sincere coming from them.

When your mother received the first two big letters from you recently, she called me immediately and read them both in their entirety. As you no doubt are aware, for months they had no idea of the nature of your situation. They were forced to depend on rumor, conjecture, and, worst of all, innuendo. They survived all this torture with admirable courage and have been rewarded in turn. I assure you that your letters have brought them back to life.

You did not make mention of the possibility of your return during the course of December. If this be so, then you'll never see this letter. It's been over a year since we've seen one another and almost exactly six months since you began your Cuban sabbatical. I pray that there will be no problems and that you will be home by Christmas. If not, hang in there.

There is little to say of my situation except that I am surviving and that this is no time to compare our problems. I'm still working for the County and am relatively happy with my work. I'm still married and living at the front house on Guyer Ave. Instead of poor, I'm going into hock because I have to heat the place, insulate rafters, make mortgage payments, etc. Not the best of situations, but better than most these days.

I have strained myself to remain light and non-controversial during the course of this document, not wishing to in any way endanger its delivery. Resultantly, there is little left to say at the present time. I'm sure we can and will say it all later. In the meantime, try to console yourself with the fact that your friends and family are thinking of you and eagerly awaiting your return. I will write again.

Andy

To hear that my mother and father were holding up and surviving "all this torture with admirable courage" barely put me at ease. It was left-handed reassurance, but it was comforting to know that my friend would do what he could to help my parents deal with the difficult messages they had received during those months. Saying that I had a knack for getting out of tight spots struck me as mere fabrication to make my parents think that I had greater guile than I could ever have hoped for. His concern and thoughtfulness were even more significant in light of the events taking place in his own life; his mother was battling cancer, and the doctors held little hope of stopping its advance.

After indecision and difficulty with arrangements, on January 4, 1974, Chet went to get some treatment for venereal warts. This involved a trip to the hospital on the parapets. Although my hearing was not very good, and my Spanish fluency was hardly better than his own, I accompanied Chet as an interpreter. After being detained by guards who saw no reason for me to accompany him because only one pass was issued, we were escorted to the hospital. In vulgar slang, I indicated to the doctor that he had warts on his ass. He got the idea of what I was trying to communicate, and he found the choice words amusing. I walked outside while he conducted the examination and shortly thereafter Jeff came over from his section. We shared a smoke as Chet emerged with a grin: he had been given a script for Darvon. They would hardly alleviate his condition, but they would bring some joy to the cell when we used them later.

When we returned to our cell, we were overjoyed to find out that more mail had come. For me, it was a bonanza: two letters from my mother, one from my girlfriend in Hawaii and one from my sister. They had all been sent in November. I felt rich. The two from my mother were dated November 16 and November 17. The numbers on them indicated they were the fourth and sixth that she had sent. The news was general: she talked about my sisters Gayle and Carol-Lou and their children and activities, about friends, and about their rental units.

My mother's letters stirred up the longing for my family's warmth I had managed to push to the back of my mind. Since the letters were arriving one to two months after they had been sent, and arriving out of order, each one helped fit into a jigsaw puzzle of information.

The fourth letter was from Lorna in Hawaii, the first one I received from her.

November 19, 1973

Dear Gordon,

Thought I'd drop you a line while I have my wake-up tea. I hope all is well with you.

You know, I spent 3 months in New Jersey—had a problem arise and thought I'd better return to see if it could be straightened out. Everyone, including your parents, were really helpful. Sure is nice to know you have many good friends.

Hawaii is still beautiful tho & I hope to live here for a while.

My work schedule is slightly different now.

I've a part-time secretarial job with an architecture firm that occupies my afternoons. Then at 6–10, I work at Maiko as a cocktail waitress. It's the same restaurant I worked in last spring. I really enjoy both, plus free mornings!

This house is really a great place to live—it sure beats a high-rise apartment. Well, I have to leave now, so please take care.

Love,

Lorna

Lorna's letter left me with ambivalent feelings. She continually made flip references to the rather mundane luxuries of life in the U.S. Rather than warming my affections, the letter left me feeling that she was callous to my bleak circumstances, even though she could not have known what they were. I was fond of her but did not share the attachment for her that she professed for me. Nevertheless, it was reassuring to think that someone other than my family was concerned and waiting for me.

That evening, I wrote replies late through the night and into the early morning.

"YARD" NEIGHBORS: JANUARY 1974

At this time, we became better acquainted with Tin Tan, *El Pintor.* He looked like an older and coarse version of actor Lee Marvin, with a 3-day growth of white beard, cratered complexion, and light blue eyes. He was as friendly as anyone we met at *Príncipe.* No matter how low he was on cigarette tobacco, he would always provide us with a smoke in a pinch. His silhouette would appear at the gate in the mornings, and he would yell, "*Jet, ven aca* (Chet, come here)." He usually brought a small container of coffee with him, which he would share with us. Our stunted Spanish sometimes made communication difficult, but usually, we could convey ideas to one another. When Tin Tan had visits with his family, he would share some of the food they brought. He never asked for anything in return, although on one or two occasions we managed to surprise him with a whole cigarette we had found. By his reaction, you would have thought we had wheeled out a Thanksgiving dinner with fixings.

The monotony of the days was sometimes interrupted by a voice coming down an airshaft—Jeff up on the roof. He would stop by the airshaft about once a week and bring us any news that had traveled to the hospital. One day he told us he had been working on arranging our escape with one of the friendly guards named Gallant. Jeff had promised Gallant—who wanted to accompany Jeff on his escape—$1 million. He had deceived Gallant into believing that the U.S. was indeed the legendary land of milk and honey. Despite my doubts about such an escape plan ever getting anyone more than a few miles away from the prison, I began collecting string and canvas fibers and twisting them into strands for rope.

Immediately adjacent to our cell was another cell into which ten *maricónes* had been moved. In the past, we had had little contact with them, as we had not been out of our cells for any extended periods. Now we were allowed out for almost whole days; usually, we were not locked up until shortly before the work crews and bakers returned. We were even permitted out of our cells at night. For me, this was an exceptional pleasure as I occupied much of the night hours studying the Caribbean constellations. Sometimes, I even saw the movements of satellites across the sky.

It made me think about the Cubans' allegations concerning "Spylab," the highly touted U.S. scientific experimental space station, Skylab, and the Cubans' constant paranoia.

The *maricónes,* always eager for conversation and opportunities to flirt with the "exotic" *Americanos,* would come over and try to start a conversation. Once, as I surveyed the night sky looking for navigation constellations, they began to look up as if they knew what I was looking at. One of the ghastlier *maricónes* approached me. His entire beard had been plucked, along with most of his eyebrows. His prominent nose and face were heavily powdered and he was wearing eyeliner. He looked like a ghoul, but he was merely aspiring to a beauty that was essential to his happiness. I was certain he saw himself as a woman trapped in a man's body.

As he sauntered over and tried to make small talk, he asked what I was doing. I mentioned in Spanish, "*Me gusta las estrellas.*" (I like the stars.)

"*Mi tambien,*" he said gleefully, showing a quick and simple mistaken grasp of what I meant. He started to name all the stars he thought were most beautiful.

"*Me gusta* Rita Hayworth, Loretta Young *y* Susan Hayward," he said.

During this time, one of the Cubans found us several books in English, a great fortune, especially since the real treasure was the Encyclopedia Britannica's *Book of the Year 1955*. This book was rarely out of use by one of us. The other two books were less absorbing: *Steamboilers* and *Concrete Reinforcing Forms*. If for no other reason, they were good sedatives when one wished to get to sleep. Chet and Robert, being more technically minded, gave them more than passing attention.

I started to stay up late into the night, writing letters to friends and relatives. My imprisonment even began to have a tragic allure, like something from the great poets of the Romantic Era. Being held inside an 18th-century castle made me think of the poems and lives of Keats, Shelly and Byron, the poets I had enjoyed studying the most in college. I spent long hours reflecting on fate and memories. My fantasies became more pronounced: in the early hours of the morning, I tried to use astral projection to lift my out-of-body self above the walls—floating upward effortlessly and touching down lightly on the ramparts. I could almost feel the wind blowing through my hair as thunder filled the sky and bolts of lightning struck around my feet. Like a ghost from *Hamlet,* I envisioned myself walking the parapets of the castle garbed in a dark cloak.

After staying up until near dawn, I would fall into a deep sleep, which would be interrupted by the morning breakfast of *café con leche* and *pan*. Then I would spend hours in a semi-conscious state, filled with erotic thoughts and memories. The hours of physical passion from long ago, which had once been taken for granted, now became nostalgic memories that I burnished in my daydreams.

My fantasies became more elaborately embellished, entailing a progressive, sensual ritual I created. One I named "The Satin Torment." It involved consensual and symbolic bondage using satin sashes attached to wrists and ankles before applying light and sensual touches to the feet, waist, arms and fingers, before gliding to ears, nape, nipples and navel. Then the more intense and invasive kisses, strokes and penetrations. I anticipated developing shared consenting fetishes when I could return to the arms of a lover.

These mental excursions took me to gauzy memories beyond the oppressive gray walls, ceilings and floors. Always, the sounds of the cell and the reality of my circumstances brought me back to my current fears and worries.

By now we had begun to formalize plans to make the Cubans take us more seriously and address our issues. We intended to go on a hunger strike to emphasize the injustice of our treatment. One day we were surprised to hear Will's voice from the airshaft leading up to the hospital. He told us that all the other Americans had been taken to *La Cabaña* where they were living in a real hole, a genuine dungeon. He had been transported to *Príncipe* for X-rays as he had broken his hand in a fight in the cell. We told him of our intentions to begin a hunger strike in four days and that we were going to demand to see the Swiss and protest our conditions. He said he would tell the American gang back at *La Cabaña* when he got back. He was doubtful, though, that they would take part in such a protest.

While we waited for the days to pass until we began to reject our food, we spent a great deal of energy trying to get The Louie to take part in the strike. Eventually peer pressure convinced him that his holding out would weaken everyone's sacrifice.

I also decided to write another letter to my mother.

January 7, 1974

Dear Mom,

Madrugada (the time between midnight and dawn)

I finally received my first letter from you less than a week before Christmas; 3 days ago I received one from Gayle, one from Lorna and two more from you; all were dated between the 15th and 16th of November. I don't think I can tell you how much they've helped me and how they diminished this feeling of isolation.

My health has been tolerably well, but my hypochondria has been acute. If we can see the Swiss officials soon, I hope to get some vitamins, which should help cut down on the number of colds I've contracted.

The food? *Que sabroso!* (How flavorful!) It would better suit my palate if they issued a bottle of LaChoy each week. What would I like when I return? A lot of greens, fruits and the entrails of 6 of Mike's submarine sandwiches.

The house fiberglassing sounds good; I'm glad to hear that the garage doors were changed. It should be a major improvement. What colors did you use?

Is Andy living in Lavallette or Farmingdale now? Is he still doing probation work? Please let him know that my future courses will require readings from Alex Solzhenitsyn & Orwell.

Lorna's note was brief—mentioned she was in N.J. for 3 months due to some kind of a problem. Do you know what it was? When was she there?

I'm glad to hear that you got your driver's license. Your handwriting looks very good. How come you're so good at being persistent, and I'm so obstinate at being stubborn?

Dec. 18 we went to the Revolutionary Tribunal, and we are now awaiting the verdict.

I'm optimistic and pray that I shall see you all soon. I've been a stranger in a strange land too long.

With the few materials available, it's difficult to utilize the time here in the Prince's Castle. I'm getting pretty good at reading the few newspapers & magazines we get to look at occasionally, but I've got a long way to go with conversations in Spanish. Seems that I can talk fairly well, but I have a lot of difficulty hearing what they say.

As far as the rest of the time, I'm concentrating on portraits taken from photos. I'd appreciate it if you could send me some photos of my nieces and nephews & the rest of the family so I can practice on someone I know.

Well, I must close for now. Please take good care of yourselves. Perhaps we'll be together again soon.

Love,

Gordon

During the ensuing days, we met the amazing Juan Copoz Barriera. He was quickly nicknamed *El Conejo*—the Rabbit—for his quickness at avoiding detection by the guards when he was somewhere he was not supposed to be. He spoke a smattering of English, but in the presence of other Cubans, he refused to speak anything but the most elementary level of English. His distrust for the Cuban *chibas*—rats or stool pigeons—was strong; he sensed them everywhere. He had been imprisoned five years earlier for joyriding in a "borrowed" car when he was only 18 years old. He was a combination of philosopher, magician, actor and teacher and could easily have been an entertainer with his diverse talents and charm. His eyes glinted with life, and his smile was easy and natural. He would magically appear from behind a column, which had been under steady scrutiny for minutes. He would stroll out with the confidence of a dandy—all he lacked was a cane and top hat. Whenever he spoke, his eyes lit up with an intensity that transcended the words and left one pondering the experience. His pet phrase was, "time to time, time to time." This phrase had profound significance for him; for me, it was a source of befuddlement. It encompassed his philosophy that all things must change. I could only conclude that he believed one day his acts of kindness would be transmitted either to him or someone close to him. He would bring us small containers of coffee and books. On one occasion, knowing my affinity for drawing, he brought me several colored pencils.

My small gift in return was a drawing on a card of an attractive blonde. I gave this to him on his 24th birthday; inside I inscribed,

"Don't forget all the good times we had together" and signed it "Helga." It made him a hit with his cellmates who were unaware of the card's true origins.

El Conejo, perhaps more than anyone else I met in prison, impressed upon me his constant sense of being watched and overheard by the *chibas* who sought information they could barter for favors from the prison authorities.

Among our growing contingency of acquaintances was one of the stranger prisoners.

He weighed about 300 pounds, walked with a cane, had a dog not much bigger than a mouse, and spoke excellent English. This peculiar figure quickly brought to mind images of 1940s actor Sidney Greenstreet, with his polished manners that so sharply contrasted with those of the general prison populace. He went by the name of Dr. Bruni, though it was never established what he was supposed to be a doctor of. He was an epicure who would spend hours describing the dishes he enjoyed preparing. What added to his oddness was his apparent familiarity with the history of our case. He maintained, after a certain point, that he had connections in G-2. Eventually, he began to tell us that we would be released soon, but we attributed this to devious attempts to ingratiate himself with us, perhaps even to report back to the authorities. Then he asked us to send him a pair of sunglasses similar to the pair I had. Cal promised that he would gladly do that if we got released.

Finally, the day for our hunger strike arrived. Milk was delivered to the cell early in the morning and was refused. The Cubans looked at us dumbfounded, then they carried the unused container back to the kitchen. The morning passed. *Almuerzo* came and again the food was turned away. To the inmates bringing the food to our cell, this was sheer madness. By the evening meal, the section chief came by and peered in our cell, but he made no mention of the unaccepted food. The dinner meal was so foul-looking that no one felt any great loss by not eating. Our first 24 hours of fasting passed rather easily.

The next day, the largest portions of *café con leche* we had received so far were sent away and not without regrets. Lunch looked like it had been cooked in a restaurant. Our resolve remained unchanged and surprisingly, after 48 hours of not eating, none of us seemed too bothered by the absence of food. Late in the second day of our hunger strike, the section chief talked to us about why we were rejecting the food. He made it sound like we were personally insulting him. Chet told him that he was being quite fair in his treatment; however, this was an issue that involved his superiors. We did not intend to end our fast until we had seen the Swiss officials.

On the third day, even larger portions of coffee-flavored milk appeared at our cell door. The amazed Cubans who brought it to the cell walked away shaking their heads at the crazy Americans.

At noon, the section chief spoke to Chet with Dr. Bruni acting as the interpreter. He told Chet that the captains of the two boats would be permitted to speak with the Swiss the following day. We indicated that we would accept food that evening based on the section chief's assurance that Chet and Robert would see the Swiss officials the following day. That evening meal, our first in 60 hours, left us bloated and sleepy. Our anxiety of the anticipated meeting with the Swiss the following day was buried beneath the lethargy, which overtook us all.

Late in the morning the following day, Chet and Robert were called from the cell and were gone for more than two hours. During their absence, we received word through the grapevine that other Americans from *La Cabaña* were at the front gate. It appeared they had been permitted to see the Swiss also.

When Chet returned, he told us the other Americans had been brought over to *Príncipe* specifically for this meeting with the Swiss. Chet learned that our formerAmerican cellmates had united to support and take part in the hunger strike; however, they had mixed up our signals, which we had relayed through Will, and had begun their fast two days before us. This came as a big surprise. It also made clear that our actions alone had not affected those taken by the prison authorities.

Chet then recounted his meeting with the Swiss. They told him his message had been relayed to the U.S. State Department and the Swiss promised they were doing everything possible on our behalf. Chet had the impression the Swiss were genuinely glad our case had at least provided them with something they could work on. They further indicated to him they were trying to get the Cuban officials to improve our conditions. They closed their meeting by cautioning Chet that our drastic actions might not necessarily reap such fruitful results in the future. They pointed out that on Castro's island, it was not unknown for people to disappear without explanation.

Robert's meeting with the Swiss was less productive. He had been unable to learn anything about the welfare of his fiancé, other than that she was being held at the women's prison—either at *Nueva Manajay* or *Guanajay*. As he had not been to the Tribunal yet himself, there was little the Swiss could do.

We spent much of the evening in our crew groups discussing the events of the day, the impact of the strike, and our futures, which seemed as uncertain as always. All we could do in the coming days was wait, speculate, hope and pray—a lot.

WAITING & WORDS: JANUARY–FEBRUARY 1974

Whether it was because of the hunger strike or another reason, more mail arrived on January 21. There was a letter from my father mailed on November 17. It was the fifth written by my parents, but I had not received the first one yet.

November 17, 1973

Dear Gord:

Hope this finds you well. We sure miss you.

Am officially retired now and looking forward to catching up on a lot of odd jobs. There are plenty of them. We are trying to get ready to go to Florida, probably around the 10th or 12th of December.

Many people are asking for you and hoping that everything will get back to normal soon.

It is 30 degrees today, but it has been ideal weather for the past week. Atlantic City was beautiful and warm 71 degrees.

Kimberly has a birthday Sunday, so we'll understandably spend time there. They have a beautiful home.

All the lifeguards asked for you all summer. Sure miss you. Even Dick Hoffman asked for you regularly. They had a good summer.

Well, Gord, I will close for now. Would sure like to hear from you.

Love,

Mom and Dad

I also received a letter from Chet's wife. It, too, was sent in November. I think she was trying to cheer us up, but all her fears and insecurities seemed to spill out of the sentences.

Tuesday, November 13, 1973

Dear Gordon,

I was very happy to hear from you and I would like to thank the Cuban (?) who let it get to me. Also, I hope they will let you have this so you will know what I've done with your stuff.

Yes, I have been in regular contact with your parents and Lorna. They will be moving down here on Dec. 10.

As for your apartment. I moved everything out and made our breezeway into a room for you. I will try to get everything done that you asked.

Lorna will most likely write but know this, Gordon, that girl loves you a lot. You haven't been forgotten; none of you have and please don't think you have. I know it's hard being there but hold on and don't give up faith. I just pray you are okay and the rest of you too.

Gordon, I can't tell Chet how I really feel it would upset him, but things aren't going well with me. I think I'll be ending up in the hospital soon from a breakdown. I try so hard to be calm but when I think of where you all are and how long it's been, I go into a frenzy. I can't even think straight anymore. I've tried to kill myself twice but didn't get anywhere. The folks don't understand so I just sit in the house day in and day out doing nothing. I know I shouldn't say these things because all of you are in a bad way also.

But just know I understand.

Gordon is Chet okay and you also?

I pray that they will let you all come home soon.

I'm sorry but I can't write any more now I'm getting too upset. I'll write again and it will be a happy letter, OK? I love you and pray you'll be home soon.

Love,
Mona

Time dragged on painfully. Despite being engulfed by anxiety, the day-to-day living seemed better than when we were cooped up with 400 prisoners in *Once*. We got to spend lengthy periods in the sunshine almost daily as our cell door was left open the entire day and much of the night. This went on uninterrupted for several weeks until a group of prisoners on a work project were lodged at *Príncipe* for several days. As they lined up for their two daily meals, they would peer in and gawk at the odd Americans as if we were made of a different substance than they were. Once they were relocated, we were given back our rather informal confinement conditions.

On January 28, I received a barrage of letters from home: three were from my mother, one from my father and one from Lorna. They'd all been dated between November 13 and December 12, 1973, and included the first two my mother had sent early in November.

Tin Tan continued his daily visits and always kept our minds from slipping into morose speculation. Jeff had even more frequent contact with us, and he introduced us to one of his friends, Peter, *El Tifi* (the thief). He stood over six feet tall, unusual for a Cuban, had striking features, and a beautiful singing voice. He, along with one of the guards, introduced us to a number of Spanish songs that we became fond of. Among them were several by Nino Bravo, a singer from Spain. On the threshold of major international fame, Bravo died from injuries after a car accident in April 1973.

His songs, including *La Puerta del Amor* (The Door of Love) and *Un Beso y una Flor* (A Kiss and a Flower), were strikingly beautiful, both for their melodies and lyrics. Upon our repeated requests,

Peter would sing them with his happy and infectious disposition. His Spanish ramblings of anecdotes and jokes needed little translating with his animated manner.

Often he would procure coffee and food from the kitchen or other parts of the prison. When asked where he got them, he would surreptitiously flutter his fingers and proudly state he was, *Un Tifi* —insinuating he was in a league with the world's finest pickpockets. Our hours together with him were filled with pipe dreams of bringing him to the U.S. where he could find things of higher value worth stealing. He imagined the U.S. to be a place of plenty—the promised land of milk and honey—where everyone lived in splendor.

Another of the stream of acquaintances we made during this time was referred to simply as *El Mexicano.* He was about 5 feet, 4 inches tall, and had the face of a Chihuahua. He had come to Cuba in the early 1950s and worked as a taxi driver escorting American tourists about the streets of Havana; often taking them to the sleazier parts of the then sin-filled "open port." Entertainment included nightclubs where anything would go, including staged sex shows. His English was good, and he must have learned early in his cabbie days that the better he spoke it, the more of an asset he was for his fares with pockets full of cash. Frequently he would speak of the prurient interests "Old" Havana afforded—cheap prostitutes, wild sex shows, drugs and pornography. His demeanor aroused my distrust, but we stayed on casual and amicable terms. Undoubtedly he was a shrewd *chiba* playing the angles for his benefit.

One of *El Mexicano's* favorite jokes was about Superman.

"Once," he said, "after Fidel Castro took over the island, Superman came to Cuba for a vacation. After enjoying several days on the beautiful beaches and having several good meals, he said goodbye to the friends he had made and attempted to take off. He did not move an inch. Superman thought he must have had too good a time and exhausted himself. He tried to take off again with the same results.

He looked behind him and discovered that everyone on the island was holding on to his cape—each wanted to hitch a ride."

As the days trickled by, the population of the prison continued to decline, though in much smaller numbers. The seven of us became more and more restless. Jeff came down from the hospital one day and we had something of a party during his visit. It was remarkable how injecting one new person into the group could liven the mood, especially when it was someone like Jeff, who was a natural observer and storyteller.

When it was time for our cell to be locked, Jeff talked Cal into coming up to the hospital with him. He had some kind of a spare pass to get past the guards, so Cal used it to make the trip up to the dormitory section of the hospital where Jeff had promised an evening of television. We figured the overall tally of the cells would show no one missing if Cal was counted upstairs so we foresaw no problems with this deviation from the normal procedures. One oversight prevented this harmless scheme from remaining a secret.

When we lined up for the nightly count of our cell, the guards simply counted what they wanted to count: they expected to see seven people, so they counted seven, even though there were only six of us in the cell. When Cal was also counted upstairs in the patient's garb, which Jeff had borrowed for him, the total number of prisoners in *Príncipe* was one more than it should have been. They actually had one more prisoner than they were supposed to. A recount was taken. They counted six of us this time; however, Cal had gotten nervous during this count and hid from the guards. Now they were short two more prisoners than their previous count. The Cuban guards were perplexed how their counts were coming up with too few after having one too many. The third count of the night resulted in Cal coming forward and telling the guards he was in the wrong place. He was returned rather abruptly to our cell, but surprisingly, no disciplinary actions were taken, more than likely because the guard's inefficiency would have come to the attention of their superiors. All in all, it provided a break in the tedium of daily cell life.

Each day Dr. Bruni would come by our cell and ask how we "boys" were doing. He continued to insist that we should not take any further actions like our hunger strike, as he was certain we would be leaving Cuba soon. After he was permitted to leave the prison on a weekend pass, he returned to reinforce this notion, indicating that his friend in G-2 had led him to believe we would not receive a prison term. As usual, we thought this was little more than hogwash. When we gave Cal his address so that a pair of sunglasses could be sent to him, I began to wonder.

We had gotten to know most of the regular guards on patrol outside our cell during the night. Among them were two who stood out. One also sang Nino Bravo songs so well that we nicknamed him *El Cantador*—the singer. The other was *El Rojo,* the red, who would spend hours arguing the merits of the Communist system in Cuba. He appeared to have no concept of the limited nature of information the government permitted him to see. The concept of censorship and propaganda seemed entirely alien to him.

One of the conversations I had with *El Rojo* concerned baseball, probably the most popular sport in Cuba. When I mentioned that quite a few Cubans played ball for professional teams in the U.S., he dismissed them because they were paid to play. Although there was merit to what he said, he refused to acknowledge that their skills could compare with those of the Cuban amateurs. Despite his sometimes-myopic view of politics and sports, he was a likable guy. It bothered me, though, that he did not have the opportunity to examine issues from at least two points of reference.

Early one morning, before the sun came up, The Louie called me to the cell door and told me that Juan Copoz Barreira's number had been called and that he would be leaving *Príncipe* shortly. The Rabbit was to come back in a few minutes and wanted to say goodbye.

I waited by the cell door in my half-asleep state for 10 minutes as The Louie went back to bed. One of the more obstinate guards was on patrol that morning, and I expected him to give us trouble if the Rabbit and I tried to talk. To make matters worse, the guard made a point of stationing himself just outside the cell door while he smoked a cigarette. Despite the anticipated movement of several prisoners, the corridor, which ran between the banks of cells, was deserted. I stared dully at the column directly across from our cell. Finally, the guard put his cigarette out and began to walk to another section of the prison. Magically and fluidly, The Rabbit strutted from behind the column I had been staring at for the last five minutes.

He approached me and said, "I'm leaving in a few minutes." I was lost for words. Our acquaintance had been short, but we had developed strong feelings of friendship. I wished him good luck. In the Cuban fashion, we shook hands, retaining our grips for several minutes, as we talked on further. We each realized we would probably never see each other again. He wished me luck as well and said his customary "time to time." He vanished behind a column and never reappeared.

I spent that morning in a melancholy reverie. I thought of the day that I might return to a free Cuba and meet again with Juan Copoz, to a time when a conversation did not consist of periodic looks over one's shoulder to see who might be listening or watching, to the day when our lives were not so controlled by external forces.

On January 28 the Cuban officials brought us a bundle of letters. Six of them were for me. A few were written after letters of mine had been received, so there was finally a measure of feedback on what I had written. Also, the first two letters my mother had written were finally delivered. It struck me as ironic that in my mother's own way, she implied that I had not been trying to write. Otherwise, her letters were chatty and full of news of family and friends and encouragement for me.

I continued to feel deep pangs of guilt when she mentioned how she wished I were around to help. But her comment about Lorna alarmed me for reasons I had not expected.

It was my mother's distinct impression that Lorna felt I was in love with her and was intent on marrying her whenever my release took place. It was nice to know that someone was waiting for me at home, but I had no intention of leaving one prison and walking into another one with open arms.

December 10, 1973

Dear Gordon,

Since I've finished my work for the day I thought I would type you a letter, especially since it is faster than writing, and I neglected to write over the weekend. I hope you are well and that this mail is reaching you. I haven't heard from Mona or your parents lately, so I am assuming the situation remains the same.

Everything is fine here. I am now getting into the Christmas Season's rush—it is exciting in some respects but my whole being isn't into it this year. I even question whether I should bring up the subject to you as I don't want to bring you any sad feelings. Perhaps you will be home by then.

Guess what I went and did—cut off my hair. Now please calm down and don't get too excited over this news. It is still long, I really only had a few inches cut and it now has a style—if you can call it that. It is cut shorter in the front and gradually gets longer and makes a point in the back. It looks pretty good and is much easier to handle. Prior to my exposure to the scissors it was to my waist—believe me I looked about 18, not that I look any older now, but I feel better and that's what matters.

As you can gather from the above paragraph I haven't changed too much. I still ramble and don't make too much sense. You will have to forgive this letter as I am in a somewhat rambunctious mood. Oh, oh, just committed a mortal typing sin—made a hole in the paper. Tough!!!

Reading this letter over I wonder what makes you even have anything to do with me. But I'm glad you do because it makes me feel like a person and someone who has some importance in this world. God only knows the things

I too have to speak to you about when we are together again. That should be some reunion!!!

Well, my love, I shall finish this literary disaster by wishing you all the best. I pray every day for you and have even re-established my relation with the Catholic Church on Sundays. If the Man can't do us any good, who can? With all my love from head to toe, every drop I have to give you, I will close till next time.

Lorna

After receiving such letters, and reading and re-reading them several times, the whole scope of life seemed so great. The frivolous aspects of day-to-day existence as I had lived it became magnified. My previous indulgences brought about a revolution in my thinking and beliefs. I became determined to appreciate each of my friends with the caring that I felt people were extending to me in my unfortunate circumstances. In such an unlikely place—a subterranean cell on an island that had little direct contact with the rest of the world—I saw for the first time the egotism I must have displayed.

Unbeknownst to me, a lot was going on back in the States on our behalf. Although my father was not very politically active, his work brought him in regular contact with influential people who carried the banner for my release because they respected him.

February 1, 1974

House of Representatives,
Washington, D.C. Rep. Charles W. Sandman, Jr.

Dear Ben:

Just wanted to update you on the Gordon Hess case, although I understand that Mr. and Mrs. Hess have retired and moved to Florida.

The four men recently were tried and sentencing will take place in the near future. I would like to mention however, that two Officers from the Swiss Embassy spoke with the men prior to the trial, and were present through the trial, and reported a number of discrepancies and inconsistencies in their stories, so it's very difficult to tell just what the outcome will be.

I do understand, however, that it was recommended by the court that they each receive a four year sentence for one of the charges, and a two year sentence of the other, making a total of six.

Sorry this one has taken so long, but some of these cannot be rushed. With all good wishes, I am

Sincerely, Charles W. Sandman, Jr.

Time moved by slowly as we awaited a decision from the Tribunal. We began to talk of a new hunger strike: this time for our freedom. We did not expect it to be over in just a few days. This time we anticipated it testing our resolve to the fullest. We finally agreed to wait one week before we would begin. I spent the time sketching and on February 20 I received several letters from Lorna.

February 20, 1974

Dear Sunshine,

How do you like your new nickname? It came to me one night while listening to *You are the Sunshine of My Life*. Please let me know if you like it or not, so I can keep using it or change it.

Today through all the Hawaiian rain your letter brought the sun.

I, too, think of you often, almost constantly and pray for your soon and safe return. To say I miss you just doesn't convey my desire for your presence. I only hope over the miles you can feel my vibrations.

I like your sketch—looks really cozy & comfortable. I wonder if the Hawaiians are ready for such a modern concept.

Also today's mail brought copies of 2 of your letters to your parents. They called me on Sat. & read them (dated Aug 26 & Sept. 23). Both are well—as a matter of fact I received a letter your mother wrote 2 weeks ago, which gave your address.

Thank you for the birthday wishes.

Mona, your parents and I have been in close contact. They've been really great about calling or sending information. While I was home I called your parents weekly & saw them several times. Everyone's been very helpful—even people you may never know.

I'm sending you some lyrics with more to follow. The sentences are squashed together so as to get the most out of a page. If there are any in particular you'd like, please tell me. If it helps at all, I'm more than happy to do it. I only wish I could do more. Oh, sorry if some of the words aren't exact, but I couldn't get them all clearly.

Take care of yourself and come home soon. I love you,

Always, Lorna

January 5, 1974

Dearest Gordon,

My attempts at beginning this correspondence with novel or witty comments aren't succeeding. I do hope you are well and have received some mail from us.

My main concern is that you know how much and often we think of you. Also that we are doing everything possible to bring you all home. Somehow, hopefully soon, it will all fall into place and this nightmare will end.

How I wish this would reach you like yesterday so as to ease your mind. So many thoughts and imaginings run through my brain of how you are perceiving things, what you are thinking & feeling & what your physical accommodations are. This mail thing really frustrates me as I get the impression you feel deserted or that something's wrong. Neither are true. Yet all this while you have to wait for this & other letters to tell you all is well & while you're waiting you're thinking those things.

That's a pretty poor description of my feeling so I think I'll close now, Gordon.

There are too many things I wish to say and can't express properly in writing. Please just know we all care and are here & haven't forgotten you.

With a love that grows deeper each day, I remain Yours, Always,

Lorna

Hesse 12-73

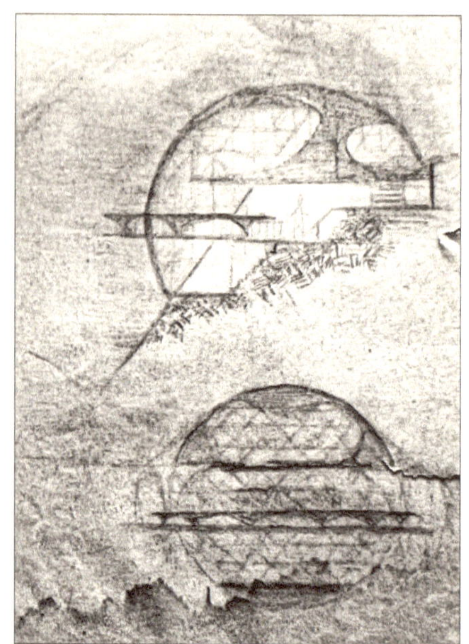

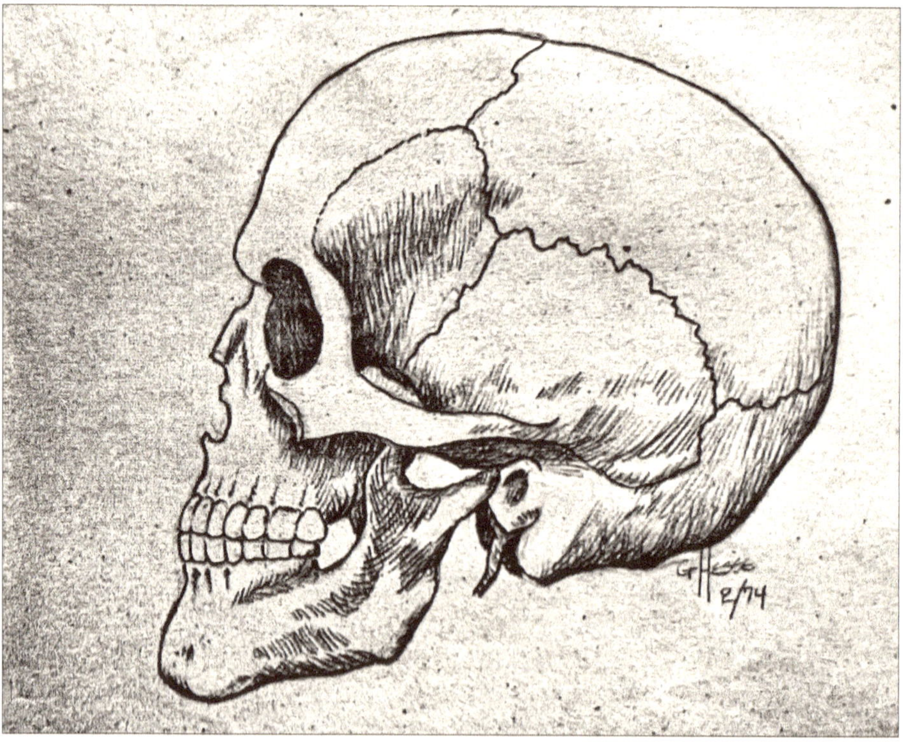

To pass the time, I sketched and drew images from memory, from illustrations on books passed around among the prisoners, and in the case of the young woman, from a photo of a fellow inmate's daughter. I even used some of my architectural training to sketch buildings and dome houses for use in Hawaii.

One evening we took a few of the Darvons that Chet had been prescribed. On an empty stomach, they were more potent and afforded a soothing sense of well-being. I would lie on my bed, beneath a sheet that served as a mosquito net and emotional cocoon. I'd imagine myself listening to the well-remembered sounds of my stereo as a record would drop onto the turntable, the needle arm would settle into the groove with a soft crackle and the Rolling Stones' *Their Satanic Majesties Request* would issue forth.

Phrases of loneliness and alienation rang in my mind:

"Mommy and Daddy,
. . . hope you both are well,
Please come see me,
In the citadel"

Then I would feel the utter desolation and sense of remoteness of

". . . It's so very lonely,
You're 1,000 light years from home."

Though I was often challenged when trying to recall lyrics, the instrumental sections of these songs sounded as clear as a bell in my mind. The Darvon-induced state brought vivid dreams while I was still awake. The pills and the imagined music made the whole situation more bearable.

Chet and I would usually interrupt the musical portion of our programs with conversations about our college days and the Clayburn House. There, within sight of the Blue Ridge Mountains, we felt far removed from the mainstream of the exciting and sweeping events that were taking place in the big cities across the country. A small nucleus of our friends who took an interest in these events had been drawn together and lived at the Clayburn House. Although there were unusually contrasting personalities, we had lived a harmonious and secure life during those days when exams, term papers, grades, and the inevitable military draft were the dominant worries. Reflecting on these days, huddled over a hand-rolled cigarette, Chet and I would contemplate the dozens of interesting people we knew and the strange events of our lives that had brought us to this cell, far removed from those happy days.

After college, Chet, most of our friends and I drifted to California; at that time, it was a mecca. We had lived in California at different times, but we both came away disillusioned with our vague and unfulfilled expectations. We had returned to our native areas and settled into the dull responsibilities of earning a living and finding careers that would provide the satisfaction for which we yearned.

When the conversation turned back to the music we had both associated with, we would usually return, wordlessly, to our respective cots and resume our semi-conscious dreams, slowly drifting into a state of peaceful rest, far removed from the reality of our situation, with the hope that tomorrow would be better.

NIGHT CALL: FEBRUARY 27, 1974

We began our second hunger strike on February 25, 1974. It had been two months since we had appeared before the Tribunal and more than a month since we had seen the Swiss consulates. If we were going to be released, we saw no reason for such a long wait, and we were ready to go at the drop of a hat. We collectively felt that the apparent uncertainty of the Cuban officials would become more decisive, either for better or worse, if we demonstrated our resolve and conviction that we were being held unjustly.

We sent a letter, written in English, back with the morning breakfast supply of rolls that said we were going to stay on our strike until we were released. To underline our determination, we accepted the morning *café con leche,* anticipating that after one month, if our demand for liberty had gone unanswered, we would refuse all liquids except water. The crew of the *Breeze Dream,* whose hopes for release were far slimmer due to the hashish that had been found on board their boat, participated in our strike out of sympathy. Despite our frequent differences, which on at least one occasion had reached the point of physical confrontation, their support in this grave matter was a powerful gesture. My thoughts were disjointed as we entered our second hunger strike, and I felt a deep existential remoteness from everything that had been familiar.

By the second day of our strike, after we had been given more letters from home—obviously an attempt to appease us—the section chief came to our cell to find out what the strike was all about. Our English-written letter was a deliberate attempt to bypass dealing with the lower-ranking officials. We wanted to contact those unknown individuals who had some authority. We refused to speak to the chief other than to say the purpose of our refusal of solid food.

The following evening, February 27, two guards came to the mouth of our cell and called our names, taking us completely by surprise. We were told to grab our things and come with them. The childhood fear of darkness swept through me. Despite one of the guards joking manner and the words *"Libertad,"* our movement from the prison at such a late hour hardly met our expectations of how we might be set free.

Overlooked previously, we quickly exchanged addresses with the members of the *Breeze Dream* and wished them good luck.

We were conducted to the main gate of the prison where we were given our street clothes, which we had not worn since July. The sight of these clothes lifted our spirits, but did not remove the doubts about Cuban intentions. Our personal items were brought to us in manila envelopes; however, my Seiko watch was missing. When we were told to get in the awaiting *aula,* I refused to leave the prison until my watch was returned. Convinced that our freedom lay just around the corner, both Chet and Cal said to forget about the watch. I told them I attached strong personal value to it and wanted to wait until it was returned. They were afraid that any delay might change the Cubans' minds about releasing us: I was certain the guards were just feigning the search, hopeful that we'd give up. I stood my ground.

After 30 minutes, my watch was returned, and it never felt better on my wrist; I began to feel less like a prisoner. I then walked over to the *aula* carrying my sea bag.

The *aula* did little to arrest my fears that we were going to be returned to G-2 where we might be interrogated separately until we had signed new and complete "confessions" of our lies before the Tribunal. Administration of Sodium Pentothal (truth serum) loomed as a possibility at this point.

The four of us traveled in silence down the dark Havana streets. Each of us was filled with a mixture of fear and suppressed hope. We peered out at the dimly lit buildings as they streaked by, and I began to smell and feel the presence of the sea. Our hearts lifted as we approached the Immigration Building.

But our hopes were dashed when we saw the different atmosphere that permeated the building and the immediate grounds. During our previous stay, the building had always been well-lit until at least midnight. On this night, only one light emanated from the doorway, and all the windows were shuttered tightly. In the past, the guards and officers had worn simple fatigues. Now they were outfitted with black Gestapo-like sashes, polished billed hats, and red star patches.

When we walked in, we were told not to say anything to each other. The downstairs reception area, which normally was occupied by several lounging seamen, was empty save for one man who said nothing. The sole illuminated lamp was adjacent to an ominously empty chair that faced a desk. Sitting at the desk was a man who had not been at the Immigration Building during our previous stay. I had few doubts, as I surveyed the changes that had taken place and the whole change in demeanor of the personnel, that we were in for unpleasant experiences. I expected to see loaded syringes being brought out on a cart at any moment.

But my fears were unfounded.

After our belongings were inventoried, and the guards who had conducted us from the prison had been dispatched, we began to talk freely. The sole lounging man we had seen told us that all the seamen who had been in the building, except him, had taken flights out to their home ports earlier that day. Dan asked the guard at the desk if there might be any food in the kitchen to eat. It dawned on me that we had not eaten in more than 48 hours. The guard looked at us skeptically as it was now almost 11 p.m., but he relented and unlocked the kitchen, bringing us crackers, jelly and potato cheese. Back in our normal, everyday lives, we would have turned the bland food aside, but now, after being without nourishment for days, it was welcome.

Each crew member was issued a Swiss protection passport to ensure safe passage to Mexico City.

Chet then spotted one of the immigration officials coming down the staircase. It was the man we labeled "George" because he was rarely without a cigar and had a slight resemblance to a young George Burns. He had told us in July that things would be okay in just a little while and that we needed to be patient. He appeared embarrassed by our presence and tried to slip by without being noticed, but it was too late. Chet cornered him and asked what was going on. The three of us watched as they conferred in a corner for ten minutes. When it was over, Chet told us that we were to speak with the Swiss officials the following morning. Despite our previous experiences, which led us to disbelieve what we were told by the authorities, our hopes began to swell. Could it be possible that the months of longing would soon be over?

We again talked late into the night, hoping and letting ourselves think—for the first time in many months—of the joy of being with our families, of returning to our homes. Our impatience grew by the hour.

SWISS: FEBRUARY 28, 1974

The next morning, Cal woke me up to tell me that the Swiss were downstairs. I tried to slow myself down as I struggled to get my pants on. After splashing handfuls of water on my face and brushing up, I scurried down the spiral staircase and saw Chet as he walked out of one of the rooms, which had been previously off-limits to us. The immigration chief held the door and Cal was called in. Chet reported that, in fact, we were about to be deported. It was music to my ears. The word deportation took on a joyous and carefree connotation. It was like winning a ticket on a game show for a "fabulous vacation." The idea of being exiled from Cuba had an indescribable appeal.

Soon I was called into the office. Two of the Swiss representatives who had been present at our trial shook my hand. In the Chief's presence, they explained what Chet had just told me. They said that it would take seven to 14 days before our papers were processed, which would permit us to exit Cuba through Mexico, which was necessary since direct flights from Cuba to the U.S. were forbidden. The Swiss began to fill out a form for a protection passport and other documents to permit our passage to Mexico City.

After this meeting, they asked if there was anything they could do in the interim to help pass the time. I asked for some books and if phone calls could be made to my family. They promised us books, but the Chief interrupted by saying that any telephone calls would have to be cleared with higher authorities. I asked what would happen to our boat and what was the verdict of the Tribunal. They said that the Cubans would keep our boat, and we were lucky that that was all they were keeping. Frankly, I did not see how they could get away with this, but after what we had been through, I really could have cared less. After all, it was not my boat; the owner could try to get it back if he chose to do so. I was told that the Tribunal rendered no verdict. It struck me as strange that the justice system that imprisoned people for more than nine months would not acknowledge the innocence of the accused.

After we shook hands all around, I returned to Chet and Cal. We were very happy—almost ecstatic. But our good thoughts continued to be marred by concerns that this time of anticipation, like the last time, could change quickly if the Cubans changed their minds.

After we had all conferred with the Swiss, we were taken for a short daylight tour of Havana and to a shop for our passport photographs. Then we were given inoculations, which were required to enter Mexico. Then the real treat: a visit to an *al fresco* ice cream parlor. What a difference one day made. Just 24 hours earlier we were two days into a hunger strike in a dark, dank and medieval dungeon with no hopes for the future.

Ice cream never tasted better than it did that day.

New acquaintances came with our new living circumstances. Shortly after our move to the Immigration Building, I met Edward, a unique man in his early 30s. He was Black, with almond-shaped eyes, and his dignified bearing connoted intelligence, keen skills of observation and quiet reserve. He was a marine engineer who was working on his father's shipping line when he was apprehended in Cuba. A Canadian citizen, he lived part of the year in Sweden.

When I first met him, he was extremely paranoid and hesitant to carry on a conversation that was anything but superficial, especially if it was inside the Immigration Building.

He had stopped over in Cuba for a day or so while the ship he was on was loaded. He inferred that it was during this time he had become involved in an unspecified "incident" for which the Cubans detained him. My guess was he might have been in Chile as the Allende regime was overthrown or had been involved with a black market trade. He told me he ended up at G-2 for several months, suffering two heart attacks while he was there. Although he did not say it outright, he suggested they had psychologically tormented him through real ordeals, as he was only 30 years old. Shortly after we met, he became panicky when he heard that we had been in the Immigration Building months previously and then had been returned to G-2 and then months of prison. He feared that such a fate might be in store for him.

Edward cloaked much of his words, as he was suspicious of everyone. Eventually, I won some of his confidence, but he still feared that any information he shared could be extracted from anyone.

One day, as we sat by the seawall after breakfast, Edward and I discussed the *I Ching*. When I referred to it as an occult oracle, he explained it offered insight into the changes that were about to take place at any given time; that empirical measurement could not account for the elements of chance or describe or predict even the shape a cloud could take in a few moments. Then he brought up his own experiences with the *I Ching*.

Edward had consulted the oracle when he was in another (unnamed) country, that was on the threshold of violent upheaval. The book had forewarned him not to meddle in affairs that did not directly concern him. But he did get involved in such affairs, and he attributed his problems in Cuba, in part, to this meddling. I could only conclude that he was referring to the recent overthrow of the Communist Allende government in Chile, an ally of Fidel Castro. If Edward had meddled, it would make sense that the Cubans would detain him once they learned of it. The severity of what he must have undergone—alone in an unfamiliar country—must have been extreme. I began to grasp how great his paranoia was when I off-handedly asked him how the U.S. Skylab program had worked out. His expression changed immediately to one of a desperate, caged animal. He told me not to say another word about anything involving the U.S. military activities, especially within earshot of the guards.

Edward struck me as a humane person who had endured entirely unexpected circumstances in Cuba. It was distressing to see a man of such refinement in continual fear. Although most of our conversations were casual and informal, there was always a strained manner about him. It was a further example of the altering effects of the Cuban government's practices.

There were two other striking individuals we met at the Immigration Building during our second stay. Both were hijackers. One we had already met at *La Cabaña*. At that time, he said his name was Tex; now he introduced himself as Jim. He told us that he had told us the phony story about being Cuban when we were getting our shaves because there were plenty of *chibas* around who were hungry for information. This struck me as being, most likely, a half-truth. Now I had more time to study him. He stood slightly over six feet, and his mannerisms reminded me of Clint Eastwood. He said he had served with U.S. Special Forces in Guatemala and now was teaching karate to students at the University of Havana.

I had the distinct feeling he lied just for the enjoyment of stringing people along, as much for sport and prestige as for any personal gain.

The other one was Gabor, a self-proclaimed patriot of the Hungarian Revolution of the 1950s, who accompanied Jim. Gabor had fled to the U.S. when the Soviets took back control of Hungary. Both men wanted us to give them some personal belongings because they were valuable on the black market. Eventually, they ended up with several of our towels, pants, socks and boots.

Gabor said he had been a freedom fighter leader in the October 23, 1956, anti Communist uprising in Hungary when he was only 17. In the following years, he hijacked a Piper Apache out of Miami on November 20, 1967, pulling a gun on the pilot and telling him to head for Havana. When the plane landed at the Cuban airfield, Gabor was rushed to G-2. His history of fighting the Communists in Hungary hardly warmed the Cubans to his plight.

From the day he landed, he was kept in Cuban prisons and jails for almost five years, almost a year and a half of which was spent in solitary confinement. He said he received injections of strange drugs while in G-2.

Gabor's life as a "free" man in Cuba paled next to his fond memories of the life he would gladly have returned to in the U.S. federal penitentiary.

"At least every morning there I could count on getting Kellogg's Corn Flakes," he would say, wistfully.

I learned that Jim had hijacked an airliner bound from Nashville to Miami on December 11, 1968, with his wife, Gwendolyn. It was nearly impossible to tell where the truth began and where it ended. He had told us that he had been arrested for the robbery of gems from a jewelry store in Phoenix and then, during his imprisonment, he had killed a man. He escaped and was forced to flee the country with the authorities hot on his trail. When he got to Cuba, he was immediately locked up, as was his wife.

Jim told us about the conditions at the women's prison, *Nueva Manajay*. His wife had been incarcerated there and had only survived by her ability to stand up to the physical abuses inflicted upon the weaker prisoners.

I suspected that both he and Gabor were placed in the Immigration Building for the sole purpose of keeping an eye on the crew of the *Silver Sands*. I suspected they were operatives of G-2, and I realized that my experiences in Cuba had ingrained me with a certain amount of paranoia.

Perhaps one of the happiest occasions for us after arriving at the Immigration Building for the second time was the reunion with Julio, the radio-listening guard. His face lit up when he saw us, and he was genuinely happy to hear of our release and anticipated return home. The days of waiting were shortened by his friendly manner in a hostile environment where hidden agendas seemed to lurk beneath the surface of every word.

DEPARTURE: MARCH 6, 1974

Chet and I sat on the seawall and studied the brilliant scarlet clouds of the sunset as we talked about the future. We could only speculate on what had taken place in Florida in our absence. We could only guess at the repercussions our experiences would have on our lives.

When the stars began to lighten, and the wind blew with a February chill, we headed into the brightly lit building. The nights passed slowly. Occasionally the one television station would feature an English movie, and this was a big delight. *Key Largo* was on one night, and the curious perspective it cast upon Cuba in the 1940s as a haven for gangsters was intriguing in light of our experiences here three decades later.

On the third day after our release from prison, the Swiss stopped by and dropped off several books to make the time pass more quickly. It was reassuring to know they were keeping us in their thoughts and working on our transit papers. Some of the books were *Our Town, Huckleberry Finn, By the Skin of Our Teeth, The Glass Menagerie, In Our Time* and *Three Sons.* I would glut myself into a drowsy state reading this literature, which no longer served the purpose of entertainment but rather helped pass the time in limbo.

On the fifth day in the Immigration Building, we were measured for clothing so we could be dressed in "proper" fashion for our deportation. They had a difficult time finding a pair of size 11 shoes for me as the Cuban standard of shoe sizing was in inches. Woe was the person with a size 10½-inch foot.

I was given a pair of Italian-style, drab-grey pegged slacks and a grey iridescent shirt.

I felt like a bush league gigolo.

However, this did further convince us that we were going to be leaving Cuba soon. It all added to our impatience and our anticipation.

Edward and I would spend an hour or two each morning talking about various topics. One day we were discussing aspects of George Orwell's *1984* when Edward mentioned he had pages from it in his room. Later that day he showed them to me and gave me a copy of the book he had secreted among his belongings: *The Penkovsky Papers*. This book was compiled from the letters written by Ivan Penkovsky, a high-ranking Russian official in the military and KGB who had handed over information to the West.

It was not the type of literature that was in wide circulation in Cuba. Just having it in your possession was enough to arouse one's paranoia. Edward loaned me the book and, several days later, after I had finished reading it, I mentioned it by name and said I would like to return it to him. After my blunder of mentioning Skylab to him, I should have had more sense than to mention the book in the presence of the officials in the building, but given the increasing laxity of our treatment, I did not. At my comment, he nearly turned purple, and later berated me for my carelessness.

Fortunately, nothing else developed from the incident. But based on my clumsiness, he seemed to lose trust in me.

As we tried to fill the days with diversions, Cal joined Jim and Gabor and associated a lot with Chet and Dan. It struck me that Cal was either a poor judge of character or he was similar to Jim, who I considered to be an encyclopedia of lies.

On the other hand, I had more faith in Gabor. He was easily 15 years older than any of us. He had begun a business with my shipmates by giving professional massages in return for pants, shirts and towels, which he would later sell on the black market. Eventually, I got drawn into the whole thing and lost my pants, literally. But it was well worth it. He was so skilled that after the rubdown I felt like I had been filleted. Though it was mid-morning, I crawled upstairs and nodded off into one of the most relaxing sleeps I had ever had. A day or two later he tried, persistently, to try to work out a deal for my watch; however, I would not part with it.

Chet had been pestering the immigration chief to make a telephone call home, stating that if the authorities were sincere, they would let us speak to our families to make arrangements for our arrival. The chief kept putting him off, but he finally brought us the news we wanted to hear. The papers permitting our entrance into Mexico had come in, and we would be leaving in two days. There was also another motive. He said we would need to pay nominal processing fees to leave. Money would have to be wired to a Cuban bank—about $150 for each of us. Cal said he'd get the money sent for all of us, and we could pay him when we got back to the States.

The Chief said we could make telephone calls provided there were no problems getting through the telephone channels. As it turned out, there were plenty of problems, but the calls got through anyway, after more than an hour of trying to complete them.

Speaking to my parents for the first time in almost a year was different than I had expected. Rather than a torrent of words, conversation transpired slowly, and in a state of shock. Again, it all seemed so unreal. My parents were okay and staying in Florida. They had not been notified of our impending release by the State Department as we had been led to believe by the Swiss; this was the first they knew of the recent events. Our conversations were short—there was just too much to be said without hours to get in-depth into the subjects, and we did not know if the calls were monitored. We assumed they were. Everything would be said later. That first call was all about hearing each other's voices and confirming we all were in good health.

Unbeknownst to my parents, the State Department *had* sent a message, but it had not been forwarded by the time I called, and they had disconnected their home phone while they spent three winter months in Florida. This was the message they had been waiting to hear ever since they learned of our predicament.

We spent the next two days on pins and needles. The desire to accelerate time was overwhelming, and I don't think I thought of anything else besides what it would be like to see my family and friends again.

Early in the evening preceding our departure, Gabor made a last-ditch effort to persuade me to give him my watch. I began to fear he would steal it off my wrist. We gave him as many things as we could spare, though that was pitifully small, and we didn't want to risk him getting caught with our belongings and delaying our departure.

Our last sunset on the seawall was an optimistic one; by the next evening we hoped to be several hundred miles beyond the lofty clouds, which we could see rising above the Florida Keys. All we could think about were our families, steak, salad, malted milkshakes, female companionship and good times—and what was an amazing, if unhappy, chapter to our lives that now was ticking away to a close.

Occasionally, a couple of young college students, who were studying English at the University, would stop in at the Immigration Building to give their lessons practical testing. They were fluent, demonstrating a surprising facility with pronunciation, expressions and idioms. The students were delighted by descriptive expressions such as, "He drinks like a fish," and "Toot your own horn." Often a new phrase would appear in the literature they were studying, and they would seek us out for an explanation. On our last evening, they stopped to say goodbye and find out what was meant by the expression "Go fly a kite."

During the conversation, I had a private discussion with one of the students. He began to talk about his family, which was now in the U.S., and I sensed his sadness that he had not seen them in more than ten years, and he might never see them again because of travel restrictions. During our conversations the previous July, he gave the impression of being a staunch supporter of the Socialist structure of government in Cuba, but on this occasion, he seemed to be harboring unmentioned emotions. As we talked, I asked him about the curriculum at the university, and he described the extensive range of literary works he studied—Chaucer, Shakespeare, Steinbeck, Hemingway, Swift, Sinclair Lewis, Dreiser and Mark Twain. He also mentioned many others, and I was embarrassed as an English major because I was unfamiliar with so many of the authors—Thomas Mann, Herman Hesse, Moliere, Fyodor Dostoevsky, Anton Chekov—and their works. In the course of the conversation, he said there was one book, however, which he was very curious about, but he could not get a copy—the Bible. This struck me as so strange since throughout the U.S., copies were abundant, available in every hotel and motel across the land, and were rarely read. And here was an individual who could not locate a single copy. It was another example of a little-appreciated freedoms.

It seemed even more interesting in light of this student's conversation with me seven months earlier when he told me that religion was for the old and superstitious, yet he was unable to explore the ideas, history and concepts of this book that was commonplace in the U.S.

Later in the evening, Dan and I were watching television when George, the immigration official, sat down. He had earned our distrust in July, during our previous stay at the Immigration Building, because he kept lying about when we would be sent home. After a few minutes of pretending to watch TV with us, George tried to draw us into a conversation with what Dan and I thought was a cheesy gambit.

"You know, you Americans have a very funny man," he said, expecting us to take the bait.

Dan and I stared stone-faced at the black-and-white television. Neither Dan nor I was particularly interested in pursuing his feeble attempt to get a conversation going and ignored him.

"Yes," George said undeterred, "He is one of the funniest men in the whole world." Dan and I gave each other sidelong glances and tried to suppress the twinge of curiosity that began to stir.

Who on Earth is he talking about, I thought. No one was *that* funny.

"In fact," George stated, "there is probably no one in the world who was funnier or loved by more people. A very funny man."

I couldn't stand it any longer.

"Who are you talking about?" I asked with annoyance.

"Ahh . . . I don't remember his name," George said with slight exasperation. Then we were hooked.

"Tell us something about him so I can remember for you," I said, frustrated.

George began by repeating that he was indeed a very funny man. Great, I thought. He said this comedian had been in numerous films and was loved everywhere. I started to reel off names that came to mind. It started to get like charades with all the promptings: Charlie Chaplin, Peter Sellers and Woody Allen.

Finally, he remembered.

"Yes, now I know, It's Harry Lauwus."

"Who?"

"Harry Lauwus!" he said proudly.

Dan and I looked at each other. Who in the hell was he talking about?

After more than half an hour of entreaties, the name began to come into focus: Jerry Lewis. Those confusing "w's" and soft "j's" had done it again.

We went to bed around midnight. Sleep had come earlier and easier for Chet and Cal. Lying in bed that night, smoking a cigarette, I thought of the events of the last 10 months; how we had been changed, physically, emotionally and mentally. We all found it hard to believe that this garish dream might soon be over. Sleep came stealthily as a gentle rain began to fall.

We were awakened early on the morning of our departure; the sun had not yet risen, and the air felt as clean as freshly washed laundry. We dressed quietly and quickly into the clothes we had been issued, deciding that it would be best to wear the out-of-style clothing made of creepy fabrics. We didn't want anything to cause an incident. Our sea bags were retrieved from a locked room and our wallets were returned to us. We were given demitasses of coffee and waited in silent eagerness for the vehicles to take us to the airport.

Two small cars pulled up, and we threw our sea bags in the trunks and got in with no farewells.

We were on our way! Was this really happening?

Then, we were speeding through the rain-washed streets, and my eyes drifted through the windows to the serene and dimly lit panorama. This was likely to be my last look at Havana. Storefronts were sparsely stocked and looked bleak and forlorn. No one wandered about the streets. Everything looked somber and colorless. I felt sorry for the people who were to spend their remaining days in a country so removed from the mainstream of international travel and exchange. I was lost in thoughts of the last year; a part of me had died, and I was experiencing a rebirth. It was March 15, 1974.

The Swiss Embassy officials joined us at Havana's José Martí Airport. We had almost an hour to wait before our flight, which we spent in a side room of the terminal building in awkward small talk with the

Swiss while the immigration chief tried to listen in, perhaps to make sure we did not mention the needs of our friends who were still in the prison. So we talked about what work must be like at the Embassy and how often they were transferred to different countries, getting the impression that Swiss officials with the least seniority were assigned to Cuba first.

Then we received word that it was time to board Cuban Airlines Flight 4645. Our hearts were pounding. We shook hands all the way around and thanked the Swiss for the work they had done on our behalf. Then, with our sea bags in hand, we boarded the plane.

Within minutes we were taxiing down the runway and then . . . aloft! And West. And yes, we were going home.

COMING HOME: MARCH 15, 1974

I looked down at the last stretch of the Cuban landscape as if in a dream. The faces of friends I had met during the last 10 months flowed through my mind—Roger, Richard, El Conejo, Julio, Tin Tan, Edward, El Tifi, El Rojo, the political prisoners—all left behind. All behind bars.

We sailed across the Gulf of Mexico. The daily issue of *Granma* was handed out with a courtesy Monte Cristo cigar, the premium Havana cigar. I stuck it in my pocket and thought of an 80-year-old friend who was a rolled tobacco *aficionado*. I planned to give it to him.

An hour and a half passed. The coastline and rugged mountains of Mexico came into view. We were to land in Mexico City, have an 8-hour layover and then fly into Miami. We began our descent as the circular shapes of extinct volcanoes slid beneath the window. The expanse of Mexico City appeared, and—finally—we touched down.

After checking with the Customs agents, during which Cal nearly caused an incident by telling people standing in line our whole history in Cuba, we raced off to the restrooms where we shed the ugly and uncomfortable clothes.

After I settled back into life in the States, I continued to sketch scenes from my Cuban incarceration from memory as a way to ease the transition and make sense of a senseless experience.

I hopped into a pair of white Levis work pants, a pullover and work shoes. God, how good it felt once more to have on clothes that I loved. Then we found our way to the public telephones.

We placed calls to our parents and told them that we were going to disembark at the stopover in Tampa, which seemed like a more logical place than Miami to end the final leg of our journey home for two reasons: We thought we might be accosted by State Department officials and the press in Miami plus Tampa was closer to our families.

Cal had had some money wired to him, and he graciously split it among us. We now had about seven hours to enjoy Mexico City. The thought of leaving the airport was alluring, but each of us seemed to be content to stay there, have a hamburger and a beer, gaze in wonderment at women, and buy a souvenir of what had turned into a bizarre "vacation."

Chet was familiar with the Mexican *dinero,* so I did most of my shopping with him while Cal and Dan went off to a bar. I bought a colorful scarf for my mother, postcards and trinkets. When we went to the bar, we found Cal and Dan both slightly drunk from their celebration. They had quickly made the acquaintance of two college coeds who were returning to Texas after a vacation in Acapulco. The girls were mesmerized by their stories of our adventures.

Chet and I got caught up in the sweep of things and started to have a few beers, which went straight to our heads. Quite soon we all had glazed eyes, particularly the early starters who were getting smashed on bourbon on the rocks.

Evening darkness came quickly and along with it our scheduled departure. About an hour before we were due to board our flight to Tampa, Chet and I started to drink coffee. It was obvious that Cal and Dan were on the threshold of needing help navigating from this point on. One of the girls had already left, but the other, given a few more hours, was likely to make lasting memories for the acquaintances she had made. It was with no small difficulty that we talked our tattered crew into boarding the ramp to our plane.

Soon we were underway. It took almost no time at all for Cal and Dan to blow the low profile Chet and I were hoping for when they started asking the stewardesses for kisses and drinks—before the plane had even started taxiing.

Fortunately, the flight attendants were kind and even sympathetic. Word got out to the pilots of the four unusual passengers on the flight, and they sent complimentary drinks back to us. Just what we needed! There was no way I intended to let my parents' first glimpse of me after nearly a year be one of a stumbling, inebriated and emaciated figure. I'd just have to be emaciated. I gave my drinks to Dan who seemed to be doing better at holding his own.

The stewardesses surprised me with their friendliness, particularly in light of our rambunctious behavior. I spent much of the flight removed from the festive atmosphere. My thoughts were far ahead of our airplane—to my parents, to my sisters and to the events that would take place when we arrived in the States. What had we missed?

During one such musing, one of the airline hostesses sat down beside me, and we had a short conversation about our interests. It was great for my ego, particularly when she gave me her address in Miami with an open invitation and a friendly kiss. As we floated through the darkness, I attained maximum altitude—at least until she told me she'd like me to meet her husband. The descent had begun.

REUNION: MARCH–APRIL 1974

Tampa's lights welcomed us. On the next page would be my parents—waiting with their usual patience. Minutes later we were taxiing to the gateway, straining to get a peek at the people inside the terminal, looking for a familiar face.

Then we were walking along the telescoping corridor ramp leading into the terminal building, anticipating the first glimpses of our families. I saw my father on the other side of a glass wall. His hair had turned white since I had seen him last. We put our hands against each other's through the glass. The intensity of the physical barrier of that partition was immense, yet the bond I felt with him had never been stronger. I saw my mother sitting in the distance. I raced on ahead to the Customs counter and dumped my belongings out in haste, spreading them helpfully to display everything, knowing there was nothing to hide, trying to accelerate the unwanted routine. Every moment apart from my parents burned with the desire to touch them, to feel the remarkable experience of being alive with people you loved more than you ever knew.

Although I always loved and respected my parents, I never fully appreciated and understood their sacrifices for me until I was trapped so far away. This photo was taken within the first week after my return.

Finally, the barriers were gone. I was with them again. We hugged, wept and kissed. It was so good. Time, which had been an enemy for so long, was now delicious. I was euphoric!

Once the flush of emotions settled, I went over to each of the members of the crew, shook hands and met their families. Emotions were incredibly high.

Quickly we bid each other goodbye. My parents and I left the airport and headed to their home near Melbourne. It would be my first visit to the modest winter home they had purchased the previous year.

When we had driven a few miles and the conversation stopped spilling out, my father asked me the question I knew would be coming, but for which I had not been able to prepare an answer.

"Gord, what were you doing on that boat?"

There was a long pause while I collected my thoughts.

"Dad, there's no way I would ever want you or Mom to need to lie because of something I had said or done."

But there was more I needed to say. Never, it seemed, had choosing the right words been more important.

"I can tell you I got on that boat because a good friend asked me to cover his back, and yes, I was seeking an adventure that I could write about. If people ask what I *told* you, you can say we were headed to Grand Cayman Island where the vessel would be outfitted for salvage operations."

There are few other things I remember about that drive; the overload of emotions has muddled the events, conversations and sensations. I felt free in a way I had never felt before. There was also a warmth and acceptance that had always been there but never had my soul needed it as much.

Almost 36 hours went by before I could sleep again. I stayed up until sunrise talking with my parents about the previous 10 months. The excitement of being home made it almost impossible to eat, and I chain-smoked like a fiend (when I was not around my mother). It was incredibly good to be home again.

St. Petersburg Times, March 17, 1974

Four Floridians Freed From Cuba

GAINESVILLE (AP)—Four Florida men held in Cuba since their shrimp boat was seized 10 months ago have quietly returned home.

Calvin Giron and Dan Halford, both 24 and of Gainesville, and Ashley Longstreet, 26, and Gordon Hesse, 25, both of Jacksonville, returned to their homes late Friday via Mexico City and Tampa.

"I wasn't sure I'd ever get out of Cuba," Giron told WCJB-TV in Gainesville in an interview Saturday. "But now that I'm back, I never knew that Gainesville looked so good."

The four men and their boat, the *Silver Sands*, had been held in Cuba since May 26, 1973.

The Cuban government said it seized the Jacksonville-based boat after finding it in Cuban waters near Nuevitas on the northeast coast of the island.

Florida Today, Monday, March 18, 1974

Trawler Crew Quiet On Imprisonment

The skipper of a shrimp trawler, who was jailed in Cuba with three crewmen for 10 months, said Sunday the U.S. State Department has told the four not to talk about their imprisonment.

"The things I could say could help or hurt other Americans being held in Cuba," said Ashley Longstreet, 26, from his home in this North Florida city. "That's why they don't want us to talk about it."

Longstreet said he did not know how many other Americans currently are being held in Cuba but added that he was housed with at least 15 at a location he would not disclose.

Longstreet, Gordon Hesse, 26, also of Jacksonville, Coolidge Giron and Dan Halford, both 24 and of Gainesville, were released by the Cuban government Friday and returned to Florida via Mexico City without fanfare.

The men and their boat, the *Silver Sands*, were seized on May 26, 1973, by Cuban authorities, who said the vessel was in Cuban waters and was carrying guns and a large amount of money.

Luke Bing of Jacksonville, the owner of the vessel, denied at the time that the boat was carrying contraband, saying it was on a trial run to test new engines.

During the days that followed, I experienced some adjustment problems from the abrupt change in living conditions. Less than three weeks earlier I had been on a do-or-die hunger strike in a clandestine system that had little understandable order to it.

Now I felt a bewildering discomfort in public places; no longer the casual and easy thing it once had been. Often I would begin to feel misplaced when I joined my parents on brief excursions to stores and restaurants; crowded places left me feeling unaccountably uneasy. Just staying at home felt more insulated, but the return to a more normal life required increasing amounts of exposure to the mainstream of American life. Medical checkups, buying clothes, getting my car re-registered and into operational mode, and similar activities—very slowly at first—gradually increased my ability to step out in the sunshine.

As friends and acquaintances learned I was home again, letters, calls and telegrams came in. Most said their prayers had been answered. I was moved and comforted to learn of the concern and care that had been extended to my family and me, and these unexpected kindnesses restored my previously failing hope about people I knew. I spent a week with my parents before they returned to New Jersey. They seemed to understand that I needed time to meditate and ponder my recent experiences and they left me at their house to give my adjusting mind and body a chance to sort out the things that had been whacked out of perspective.

I spent another week at their place, for the most part in seclusion, and was treated to the hospitality of newly acquainted neighbors, who were kind and understanding without being imposing.

A nearby aunt and uncle took me out to a fancy Chinese restaurant for dinner and avoided asking too many questions about my experience. The wonder of extended family and the power of their support struck me in a way it never had before. They innately understood the type of nurturing that would help me feel whole again, but they did it in a way that was neither coddling nor patronizing.

In the childlike state of my rebirth, this support helped immeasurably. I was seeing the world, society, people and relationships in a new and profound way.

Lorna now sent me her first message since I had been released. It was a pleasure just to know that we could speak our minds freely.

April 8, 1974

Dear Gordon,

Thought I would start this on my lunch hour as I'm usually pretty tired when I crawl in from the restaurant at night. This morning has been a rough one for me as I didn't really wake up until about 11 a.m. and my typing reflected that fact. So please excuse this if it isn't exactly up to par for a supposedly "top notch" secretary.

Since you didn't get my last few letters yet I'll try to remember some of the things I wrote, I hope you don't mind repetition.

I'm really excited about my parents coming out. I will probably take about three or four days off from work to drive them around, etc. We are going to the Big Island for one day only due to lack of time and limited funds. I hope to take them to the volcano and if possible drive to Kona. That should make you happy—then I can give you a report on my findings and if it's as good as you say. I get two reactions from people here and they run about even for good and bad things, so I have to find out for myself.

What is the status of the ear operation? Is it a top secret why you may get it for free or can you tell me? I love to talk to you even tho the phone can be a hindrance at times. But if I want to see you in the real live flesh and bone I had better restrain myself from making toll calls to the East Coast.

Rereading this letter both the typing and some of the English leave much to be desired. Wonder if the fact that it's that time of the month.

How are Mona and Chet getting along? Is she giving him as much grief as you? I really don't understand how she could do that, especially to you. My exposure to her has really been brief so I really don't have much of an opinion about her.

Everyone at home is fine and happy to hear you are back safely. In one of my letters to you I asked you if you had any ideas as to what I might do to help some of the guys who are still in Cuba. Could I write to them, and if so could you please send me names? As I mentioned to you on Sat. Senator Daniel Inouye is interested in anything you can supply, so when you've got some time or whatever, you can send your thoughts on the matter.

Also my offer to type for you still stands. If you have any notes or anything you want me to do just send it along. Since I can't really remember what else I wrote in those other letters and nothing really exciting has developed since Sat., I think I will close so I can mail this. Hope to see you soon, dear.

All my love, Lorna

My income tax refund from the previous year provided unexpected funds to help finance my return to New Jersey, and I gathered my small supply of belongings and began the long haul north. I stopped in Jacksonville for several days to gather what remained of my other belongings, and another surprise awaited me there—the deposit money from my apartment. After a short visit with the few friends I had there, I resumed the journey home.

I made my way to Columbia, South Carolina, and located friends I had not seen in several years, then I decided to visit with old friends who were living near my alma mater, Clemson University.

An unexpectedly tender welcome awaited me there. A girlfriend I had once dated—nicknamed "Chatty" Cathy—had married a good friend and lifeguarding buddy and was jolted by my unexpected appearance at their stone cabin. The last she had heard of me, I was still being held in prison in Cuba with little hope for release. She hugged me and had tears in her eyes. The gush of emotion and caring far exceeded anything I could have expected or felt that I earned and gave me a sense of value—as a person and a friend. I stayed with her and her husband for almost a week. It was rejuvenating to take walks through the woods with them, look at their crops and spend hours in warm fellowship. Each day I felt as if I was growing, both physically and spiritually.

By now I knew which questions to expect; recounting my tale felt rehearsed. But this storytelling helped purge me of many of the most negative parts of my Cuban experience, and I found myself beginning to laugh at the peculiar juxtapositions and irony of events. It struck me as odd that it wasn't until I went to prison that I got my first professional shave and first professional massage, for example.

I bid adieu sadly to these friends and began the final leg of my trek. I drove for 16 straight hours to get to Lavallette, arriving there just before daybreak. I decided to take a spin around the small town to see what changes had taken place during my year and a half absence.

A suspicious policeman stopped me within five minutes. In true small-town xenophobic fashion, he thought that my overloaded Volkswagen with Florida license plates might belong to someone who didn't belong there. It was an unappreciated hassle getting the dirty eyeball from a new policeman who was unfamiliar with me, a native son.

When he was satisfied with my credentials and story, I wearily decided to get re acquainted after a few hours of rest. I parked in the familiar driveway and said good morning to my parents as they were waking up. Then, exhausted from the long night's journey, I tumbled into bed.

Hours later I was awakened by my mother's call to come to the phone to talk to my sister. Our conversation was filled with overwhelming emotions. We talked of her children and how she had tried to explain to them why Uncle Gordy had not been able to see them during his custody in Cuba. I told her how much I had thought of her and her children during those long months; how thoughts of her daughter Kirstin playing the piano had helped me withstand solitary confinement. We arranged to meet as soon as possible that day. It was another loving reunion intensified by seeing how much her children had grown in more than a year and the delight they evoked. My other sister also appeared with her daughter, who had grown from a nursing infant into an exuberant bundle of energy.

When the excitement had died down, and everyone departed, my happiness ebbed like a tide. The high level of sustained energy and emotion drained, leaving me in a mild state of dejection. Now I had to begin to face the daily concerns, which I had been removed from for so long. I also longed for the warmth of a familiar and understanding woman.

I tried to forestall the melancholy by dropping by to see a few friends and to thank people for the things they had done on my behalf during my absence. Eventually, I ended up at the oceanfront apartment of Jim, an old lifeguarding buddy. During our conversation I mentioned Maureen, the girlfriend who used to live across the street from his apartment. We had had an affectionate relationship that ended under what I realized later were the theatrics Lorna used to keep me from leaving her. The easiest way to extricate myself from the relationship, short of being outright cruel a year and a half earlier, was by moving to Florida, a move that really was running away from responsibility and tough choices and toward the lure of the road and adventure.

Jim mentioned that Maureen had returned to the house across the street about four months before and he saw her several times a week. I asked him to mention me to her the next time he saw her. In prison, I had both dreamed and fantasized about her and began to think of our relationship, which, in retrospect, seemed idyllic. We were fond of each other, and our breakup was the product of complicated events and my failure to recognize how much I had cared—and continued to care—for her.

As I was leaving Jim's, I saw a shiny black VW turn the corner and pull into the driveway less than 200 feet away. My heart leaped. Maureen's Irish red hair was unmistakable. I fought back my hopes—maybe she has a new man in her life and no longer had an interest in me. I could think of many reasons why she would not care for me.

I yelled to her. "Maureen!"

She turned slowly and looked up. I was far enough away that she had trouble making out my features. Then recognition, followed by bewilderment, then disbelief. She could not believe her eyes.

"Gordon?" she yelled back.

I started down the stairs. She ran with arms open. My heart began to soar. She fell into my arms in mid-air exuberance and was engulfed in my loving embrace, overflowing with relief, affection and kisses. I had a profound sense of being where I belonged.

The first moments she gushed with emotion, telling me in partial phrases she had been having dreams about me; in each one, I got closer.

We would spend the night together. It was a dream come true. I was home.

Prison essentials that I held onto all these years.

EPILOGUE: JULY 21, 2024

When I returned from Cuba, after time spent resting, recharging and recalibrating my life and goals, I went on to have a successful career in public relations for several organizations in the New Jersey/Pennsylvania/Delaware tri-state area. I married and had a son who has been the light of my life.

When I recall my 10-month stay in Cuban prisons, it is the people I remember most. Of the dozen or so Americans I met and befriended there, I lost contact with all but two—Chet and Roger. Some of my fellow prisoners had been serving several years, mostly for smuggling marijuana or hijacking airplanes or boats, and the others who returned home with me simply drifted away.

Chet and I remained steadfast friends after our release and met on several occasions. He spent time as a crew member with the Mel Fischer team that found the wreck of the Atocha, a Spanish ship laden with gold, silver, and precious stones and adornments.

Later I shared a memorable night serving as guest crew on a tugboat he mastered on the St. John's River in Florida.

We maintained contact later by phone and, although he seemed troubled and hinted at some personal distress, I was stunned when I learned, right after 9/11, that he had taken his own life. It was a crushing end to a treasured friendship.

When Roger was released after completing his sentence, he lived in Mexico City and took college classes. I visited with him there for several days. We climbed a volcano, attended a bull fight, and visited the Mercado. He also arranged a blind date for me with whom I enjoyed a memorable night of Colombian music at a local club.

Roger later moved to Priest River, Idaho, where I visited him and his family. Over the years, we lost touch. Serendipitously, Roger called me just as this book was about to go to print, and we have made plans to visit again in the near future.

ACKNOWLEDGMENTS

I am thankful for everyone mentioned in *Cuban Blues* for the various roles they played in my life and to the inspiring individuals I've been blessed to know since I returned from Cuba a transformed man. I treasure every one of my mentors, colleagues and friends.

I am grateful to my friends for their encouragement and support as I worked to bring my memories to life over the past decade or more. While each individual is important, you would not be reading this book without the knowledge and talent of two of them in particular.

Brenda Lange and I became colleagues and friends nearly 40 years ago. Her writing and editing skills are surpassed only by her positive attitude, enthusiasm and commitment to helping me launch *Cuban Blues* into the world. She introduced me to Susan Shankin, the creative force behind Precocity Press, who has been the answer to my search for a publisher. Her expert guidance, creativity and insights finally turned my dream into a reality.

Both women provided the encouragement and good-natured flexibility I needed to complete this book, which otherwise may have withered on my shelves.

AUTHOR BIO

GORDON LOUIS HESSE was born in Roselle Park, New Jersey. His parents soon moved the family to the shore town of Lavallette, New Jersey, where he spent an idyllic childhood by the Atlantic Ocean.

Gordon studied Architectural Design at Clemson University before changing majors and earning a Fine Arts degree in English. While there, he was a "marginal athlete" in baseball, football, rugby and swimming and spent his summers as an ocean lifeguard in New Jersey and Florida, ultimately spending ten years as a guard.

After graduation and wanting to explore the world, he traveled to Hawaii, where he worked as a bartender, photographer, filmmaker's production assistant, deckhand and teacher. Then he joined the crew the *Silver Sands*, which is where this story begins, and where he found the adventure he had never expected.

Once home, he discovered how his experiences had transformed him. No longer a wanderer, unsure of his direction in life, he settled into a career, first as a probation officer serving as an investigator for the criminal courts and as the director of a Big Brothers-type program. Later, he became a public relations practitioner, writer, and photographer.

Gordon has published two books prior to *Cuban Blues*. *All Summer Long: Tales and Lore of Lifeguarding on the Atlantic*, a memoir of his decade of lifeguarding, and the award-winning *Island Beach:A Sonnet in the Sands* of the history in text and photos of the iconic strip of land at the Jersey Shore.

His upcoming book, *Children of the Sky: The Odyssey of Álvar Núñez Cabeza de Vaca*, is expected to be published in late 2025.

Gordon lives in the intentional community of Ardencroft, Delaware, and teaches kids how to swim at the nearby YMCA.

www.ingramcontent.com/pod-product-compliance
Lightning Source LLC
LaVergne TN
LVHW100527110826
845146LV00002B/799